The 5-Minute BIBLE STUDY JOURNAL for Women

Print ISBN 978-1-63609-615-5

Published by Barbour Publishing, Inc., 1810 Barbour Drive, Uhrichsville, Ohio 44683, www.barbourbooks.com

Our mission is to inspire the world with the life-changing message of the Bible.

Printed in China.

The 5-Minute BIBLE STUDY JOURNAL for Women

Peaceful Meditations for Bedtime

JOANNE SIMMONS

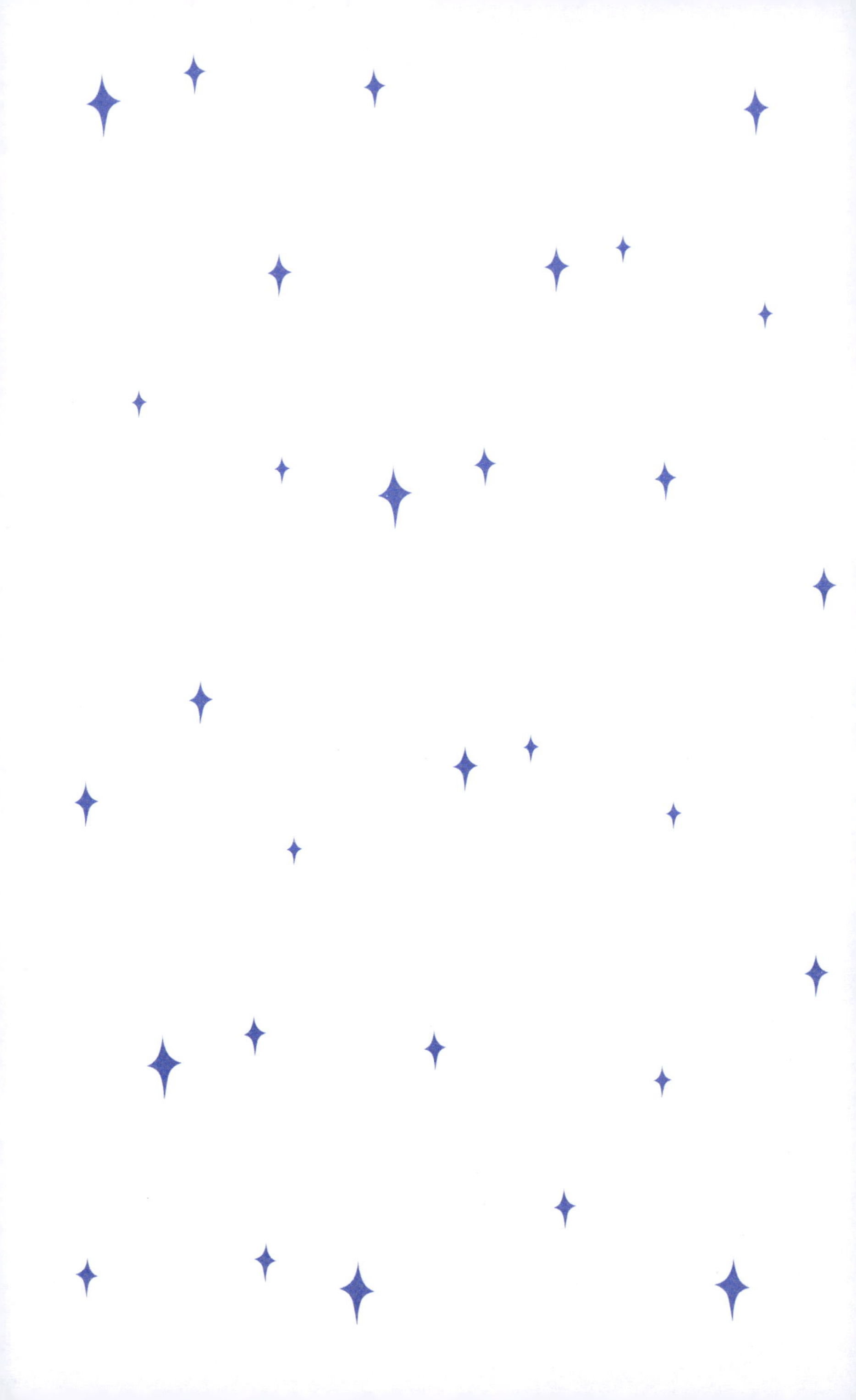

Introduction

With life whirling around you, do you find it hard to make time for Bible study? You might have all the best intentions, but the hours turn into days, and before you know it, another week has passed, and you have not spent even a moment in God's Word. Let this book help inspire you to settle down and relax, open the Bible, and reflect on a scripture passage—even if you have only five minutes at the end of a busy day!

- *Minutes 1–2:* ***Read*** *the scripture passage for each day's Bible study.*
- *Minute 3:* ***Understand.*** *Answer questions to help you apply scripture to your own life and spiritual growth.*
- *Minute 4:* ***Apply.*** *Read a short devotional based on the day's scripture to help you think deeply about the scripture passage.*
- *Minute 5:* ***Pray*** *a sample prayer that will help you begin talking to God about the scripture passage. Share with your heavenly Father—and be sure to let Him share with you too!—as you tuck in for the night.*

Let *The 5-Minute Bible Study Journal for Women: Peaceful Meditations for Bedtime* be the comforting close of your day as you focus your thoughts on the Word of God. There is no better rest than when trusting in the faithful care of your heavenly Father and loving Savior.

The Spirit Leads to Life and Peace

READ ROMANS 8:1–17

KEY VERSES:

Those who are dominated by the sinful nature think about sinful things, but those who are controlled by the Holy Spirit think about things that please the Spirit. So letting your sinful nature control your mind leads to death. But letting the Spirit control your mind leads to life and peace.

ROMANS 8:5–6 NLT

UNDERSTAND:

- *The only way to know true and lasting peace is to admit your sin nature, accept Jesus Christ as the one and only Savior from sin, and invite the Holy Spirit into your life. Have you done that? Do you have the Spirit of God living in you?*

- *When did you accept Jesus Christ as your Savior? What change and growth are evident in your life after doing so?*

- *What are the active, ongoing ways the Holy Spirit is controlling your mind?*

APPLY:

At the end of good days, maybe you settle down for the night with a satisfied sigh and a heart that feels warm and full and grateful for many blessings. But at the end of bad days, maybe you wearily crawl into your bed with a heavy, aching heart, wishing for a do-over and a different reality, wishing all the sin in the world and especially your own sin were not so real and inescapable. How precious, then, are the words of Romans 8:1–2 at the end of those terrible days! "There is no condemnation for those who belong to Christ Jesus. And because you belong to him, the power of the life-giving Spirit has freed you from the power of sin that leads to death." No matter what effects of sin you might be feeling this night, it has no power over you if you have the Spirit of God living in you. Cry out to God in lament. Cry out to God in grief. Cry out to God in confession and repentance. Cry out to God in any or all of the above. Allow Him to show you that "letting the Spirit control your mind leads to life and peace."

PRAY:

Heavenly Father, I praise You for Your Son, Jesus Christ, whom You sent to free me from the law of sin and death. Thank You for such an incredible gift! I trust in Jesus as my Savior, and I give my life and mind to be controlled by Your Holy Spirit. Please lead me in life and peace. Amen.

Lie Down and Sleep in Peace

READ PSALMS 3–4

KEY VERSES:

Let the light of Your face shine on us, O Lord. You have filled my heart with more happiness than they have when there is much grain and wine. I will lie down and sleep in peace. O Lord, You alone keep me safe.

PSALM 4:6–8 NLV

UNDERSTAND:

- *What causes you to shake with anger (Psalm 4:4)? Do you have any sin to confess because of that anger? How do you practice self-control to let God be the one to deliver justice?*

- *What does it mean to look into your heart and be quiet (Psalm 4:4* NLV*)?*

APPLY:

The New Life Version of the Bible titles Psalm 3 a Morning Prayer of Trust and Psalm 4 an Evening Prayer of Trust. They timelessly give us courage today if we meditate on them and pray them day and night as well. No matter the number or power of our enemies, they cannot compare to God's sovereign protection over our lives. No matter who is running after lies and spreading them like wildfire, God's truth prevails. No matter what is going on around us, we can lie down and sleep in peace because Almighty God keeps us safe. We cry out to Him, and He hears our prayers. He shows us what is truly right and good.

PRAY:

Heavenly Father, yes, please let the light of Your face shine on me. In a world full of evil and lies, I need to see Your goodness and remember Your truth every moment, day and night. Please lift my head when I am discouraged, and hear my prayers when I am crying out to You. I trust in You alone to give me rest and keep me safe. Amen.

God Rescues and Saves

READ DANIEL 6

KEY VERSES:

"I issue a decree that in every part of my kingdom people must fear and reverence the God of Daniel. For he is the living God and he endures forever; his kingdom will not be destroyed, his dominion will never end. He rescues and he saves; he performs signs and wonders in the heavens and on the earth. He has rescued Daniel from the power of the lions."

Daniel 6:26–27 NIV

UNDERSTAND:

- *What stood out as most familiar to you about the story of Daniel and the lions' den? What stood out as something you'd never heard of or thought much about before?*

- *Daniel 6:3 says Daniel distinguished himself among his peers with his exceptional qualities. Do you feel your faith and walk with God are helping distinguish you among others in good ways?*

APPLY:

Sometimes we think we know the most familiar Sunday school stories so well that we don't ever need to revisit them, but what better way to settle down for the night than with a familiar bedtime Bible story? It just might speak to something you're going through today. Maybe there is a way you need to continue to be faithful to our one true God, even while you fear some enemies who hate your faith. Odds are, you aren't literally about to be thrown into a den of lions, but figuratively you might feel like it. Whatever the case, be like Daniel. Never give up your loyalty to God and to obeying His Word. Never let anyone stop you from praying to Him and growing in relationship with Him. Let your heavenly Father protect you and bring justice to those who want to do you wrong. You just don't know how God might be working through a horrible or stressful situation. Like He did with King Darius, God might be using your hardship to bring powerful people to see His glory, praise His name, and urge others to do so as well!

PRAY:

Heavenly Father, no matter what concerns or dangers I might face for being faithful to You, I want to be as brave and strong as Daniel. Please use my situation to help others see Your glory and power and salvation! Amen.

Delight in God's Word

READ PSALM 119:1–40

KEY VERSES:

Be good to your servant, that I may live and obey your word.
Open my eyes to see the wonderful truths in your instructions.
Psalm 119:17–18 NLT

UNDERSTAND:

- *Do you usually delight in God's Word, or is Psalm 119 a pep talk you need to revisit regularly?*

- *What causes you to stop delighting in God's Word at times?*

APPLY:

Psalm 119 is the longest psalm and the longest chapter in the Bible. As you read the first forty verses, notice the intense theme of the goodness of God's Word—His instructions, His commandments, His perfect ways He wants us to follow. If you go on to read the rest of this psalm, you will see that theme continues. Over and over Psalm 119 describes the significance of longing for, delighting in, and obeying all God has revealed to us through scripture. As you read, take to heart the constant reminders: obeying God's commandments is the very best way to live. His rules and regulations are meant to keep us from sin and from harm and bless us immeasurably. Never let any person or ploy of this world convince you differently. Spend time reading and applying scripture daily because all of it "is inspired by God and is useful to teach us what is true and to make us realize what is wrong in our lives. It corrects us when we are wrong and teaches us to do what is right. God uses it to prepare and equip his people to do every good work" (2 Timothy 3:16–17 NLT).

PRAY:

Heavenly Father, I truly want to hide Your Word in my heart so that I don't sin against You. Please teach me, guide me, and encourage me. I trust that You always want what is best for me. I long to walk closely with You, and the more I study Your ways, the better I know You. What a blessing it is to call You my Father! I am grateful! Amen.

You Are God's and He Is with You

READ ISAIAH 43

KEY VERSE:

But now, O Jacob, listen to the LORD who created you. O Israel, the one who formed you says, "Do not be afraid, for I have ransomed you. I have called you by name; you are mine."

ISAIAH 43:1 NLT

UNDERSTAND:

- *What verses speak to you the most tonight from Isaiah 43?*

- *What are you needing to forget from the past, and how do you need God to do something new in your life like verses 18–19 describe?*

APPLY:

God's message through His prophet Isaiah to the people of Israel is for you to apply too. After reminding the people who created them and whose they are, He begins chapter 43 with a hard truth we must not forget—God never promises us a life full of cushy and easy success. Verse 2 doesn't say "*if*" you go through rivers and fire; it says "*when*" you do. Yet it also graciously promises that God will never leave you or let you be overcome by the difficult rivers and fires of life. If you ever doubt that, cling to God's priceless words to you in verses 4–5: "You are precious to me. You are honored, and I love you. Do not be afraid, for I am with you." And in the New Testament, God speaks to you through Peter when he says, "Dear friends, don't be surprised at the fiery trials you are going through, as if something strange were happening to you. Instead, be very glad—for these trials make you partners with Christ in his suffering, so that you will have the wonderful joy of seeing his glory when it is revealed to all the world" (1 Peter 4:12–13 NLT).

PRAY:

Heavenly Father, I don't want to live in fear of difficulties in life, but I don't want to be in denial of them either. Please give me peace that You will never leave me in the midst of them. You will guide, strengthen, and equip me; and You will draw me closer to You and reward me because of them. I am Yours, and I'm so grateful! Amen.

Walk Faithfully

READ GENESIS 6–9:17

KEY VERSES:

Noah found favor in the eyes of the Lord. This is the account of Noah and his family. Noah was a righteous man, blameless among the people of his time, and he walked faithfully with God.

Genesis 6:8–9 NIV

UNDERSTAND:

- *What was most familiar to you about the story of Noah and the ark? What had you never heard of or thought much about before?*

- *What do Matthew 24:37–39 and 1 Peter 3:18–22 add to the story of Noah?*

APPLY:

Have you ever found yourself on a path that you're sure God led you to, but as you keep walking it, things start feeling really strange? You're afraid you've misunderstood what you were once certain was God's crystal-clear direction. Noah must have felt that way too sometimes. He was righteous and blameless and walked faithfully with God, but you have to wonder if he started shaking his head in confusion at times when God gave instructions to build a giant boat, fill it with two of every animal on the earth, and then wait while rainwater flooded and destroyed the earth. Bewildered or not, Noah continued to obey God, and that took steadfast faithfulness and courage. In the end, God did exactly what He had said He would—He destroyed the earth with a great flood. Only Noah and his family and the animals they had gathered survived, safe inside the ark. Noah could be extremely grateful that he faithfully obeyed God whether he felt confused or not. If you find yourself trying to follow God's leading even when it doesn't make much sense, let Noah's story give you peace tonight. Let it remind you that with faithful, patient obedience, you will see God's hand and His rescue in His perfect timing.

PRAY:

Heavenly Father, please give me the peace and patience I need to keep obeying You even when I don't fully understand where You are leading and what You are doing. No matter what, I want to trust and follow You! Amen.

Powerful Prayer

READ MATTHEW 6:5–13; LUKE 11:1–13; JOHN 17

KEY VERSE:

Once Jesus was in a certain place praying. As he finished, one of his disciples came to him and said, "Lord, teach us to pray."

LUKE 11:1 NLT

UNDERSTAND:

- *What most impacts you about how Jesus taught others to pray?*

- *What most impacts you from Jesus' prayers in John 17?*

APPLY:

In times of stress, when we feel like we just aren't sure how and what to pray, we can take a deep breath and go straight to the words of Jesus when He said, "This is how you should pray." Sometimes a bullet point list is helpful to follow when our minds feel scattered and unable to focus.

- *Begin with praise to the Father.*
- *Ask for God's kingdom to come and His will to be done.*
- *Ask God to provide for daily needs without worry for needs of the future.*
- *Ask for forgiveness of sin and for help in extending forgiveness to others.*
- *Ask for protection from temptation and deliverance from evil.*

We can apply the prayer that Jesus Himself instructed to every situation and need in our lives and the lives of our loved ones for whom we are praying.

PRAY:

Loving Savior, I know I can pray to You about anything and everything, but please also help me keep good perspective and not overcomplicate my prayers, especially during stressful times. Bring me peace with the simplicity yet power of the way You have taught and have shown me how to pray in Your Word. Amen.

Rescue from the Wicked

READ PSALM 37

KEY VERSE:

Be still in the presence of the Lord, and wait patiently for him to act. Don't worry about evil people who prosper or fret about their wicked schemes.

Psalm 37:7 NLT

UNDERSTAND:

- *Do you try to be aware of current issues and news? Does it cause you anxiety? Why or why not?*

- *What does it mean to commit everything you do to the Lord? Do you feel you are obedient in this?*

APPLY:

While paying attention to the news these days, it's hard not to worry about wicked people and wicked schemes in the world. But Psalm 37 specifically soothes those fears and concerns, promising that everything wicked will soon wither away in God's perfect timing. Meanwhile, rather than fret about evil, we must focus on the good purposes and plans God created us for. It doesn't help us to be consumed with anger and rail against all that is wrong in the world. God knows, and He has a plan to end it. Our job is very simply to "trust in the LORD and do good" and let Him guide our steps. As Romans 12:21 (ESV) puts it, "Do not be overcome by evil, but overcome evil with good." It doesn't mean we won't be affected by the evil around us at times. Of course we will. But even if we stumble, God will never abandon us, never let us fall. He "rescues the godly; he is their fortress in times of trouble. The LORD helps them, rescuing them from the wicked. He saves them, and they find shelter in him" (Psalm 37:39–40 NLT).

PRAY:

Heavenly Father, please help me to never be consumed by anxiety and anger because of the wickedness in the world around me. You are the sovereign, righteous judge over all of it. Nothing will stop Your perfect plans. Guide me in the good works You want me to do, and give me peace, until one day You bring me into heaven forever with You. Amen.

In the Middle of Every Storm

— READ MATTHEW 8:23–27; MARK 4:35–41; LUKE 8:22–25 —

KEY VERSE:

When Jesus woke up, he rebuked the wind and said to the waves, "Silence! Be still!" Suddenly the wind stopped, and there was a great calm.

MARK 4:39 NLT

UNDERSTAND:

- *Do you see any differences in the accounts of Jesus calming the storm in these three different Gospels?*

- *What storm are you needing Jesus to calm right now in your life or the life of a loved one?*

APPLY:

"Don't you care that we're going to drown?" the disciples asked. We feel that frustrating question too when we're in the middle of our own storms, right? We question how God can stay quiet—*Is He sleeping on the job?* we might wonder—and not intervene exactly when we think He needs to. *Don't You care about me, Jesus?* we desperately wonder and cry too. But when the disciples asked their question, it included a false statement. They were sure they were going to drown, and that was not true. Jesus knew they wouldn't. How often do we cry out to Jesus like He doesn't care, because we're positive we know what the awful outcome will be if He doesn't come to our rescue right away? But it's a false positive. When we stop, think, and humble ourselves, we remember we surely don't know it all. Only God does. And He is perfect in all His thoughts and ways—which are far, far higher than ours (Psalm 145; Isaiah 55:8–9). Never forget that no matter what the storm is, Jesus will calm it, one way or another, in His perfect timing.

PRAY:

Dear Jesus, please forgive me when I think I know more or better than You do. Please forgive me when I accuse You of not caring. That is so unfair since You love me so much that You literally died to save me. I choose to trust that You are always working out what is best for me, even when I don't understand. Help me to patiently trust You and Your perfect ways, in the middle of every storm! Amen.

Total Transformation

READ ACTS 9:1–22

KEY VERSES:

As he was approaching Damascus on this mission, a light from heaven suddenly shone down around him. He fell to the ground and heard a voice saying to him, "Saul! Saul! Why are you persecuting me?"

ACTS 9:3–4 NLT

UNDERSTAND:

- *What is the most dramatic transformation you've witnessed in someone who has come to know Christ as Savior?*

- *Why do you think God caused Saul to go blind for a few days before beginning his ministry?*

APPLY:

If worry for a loved one whom you are praying to come to salvation keeps you up at night, take great hope in the story of Saul's total transformation. If God can change the heart of someone once so passionately hateful toward Christians that he was "uttering threats with every breath and was eager to kill the Lord's followers" (Acts 9:1), He can surely change the heart of your loved one and call him or her to saving knowledge and acceptance of Jesus Christ. Nothing is impossible for God! Throughout your days, read and study the story of the apostle Paul and all his life work to spread the gospel plus his many letters to believers. As you do, persistently pray in faith for your loved ones who do not yet know Christ that they might have a total transformation too.

PRAY:

Heavenly Father, I believe that You can work in dramatic ways in anyone's life. I pray for my loved ones who do not trust in Jesus as their Savior. Please transform them and call them to salvation in You. Amen.

Even If He Does Not

READ DANIEL 3

KEY VERSES:

"If we are thrown into the blazing furnace, the God we serve is able to deliver us from it, and he will deliver us from Your Majesty's hand. But even if he does not, we want you to know, Your Majesty, that we will not serve your gods or worship the image of gold you have set up."

DANIEL 3:17–18 NIV

UNDERSTAND:

- *Have you ever been pressured to deny or hide your faith? What did you learn from that experience?*

- *How do you plan to respond if someone ever pressures you to deny or hide your faith in the future?*

- *What are today's false gods that so many are bowing down to? How do you keep yourself from bowing down to them as well?*

APPLY:

Shadrach, Meshach, and Abednego were clearly experiencing God's inexplicable peace. How else could these three friends respond so calmly to an evil king who was "furious with rage" and threatening to throw them into a furnace so hot it could kill anyone just standing nearby (so just imagine how quickly it would incinerate anyone thrown inside!)? The friends fully trusted that the one true God of Israel was more than able to save them against all odds. They also knew He might decide *not* to save them from the blaze, and they were calm and peaceful about that too. Be sure not to miss that. They knew without a doubt that God could save them, "but even if he does not," they said, they would never serve or worship any false god. Their hope and peace transcended anything of this world because they trusted in the Most High God who transcends everything. And God did save them in such a miraculous way that not even a hair on their bodies was even slightly singed. Even evil King Nebuchadnezzar said, "Praise be to the God of Shadrach, Meshach and Abednego, who has sent his angel and rescued his servants!" (Daniel 3:28).

PRAY:

Heavenly Father, I want to calmly and peacefully trust You even in the face of extreme danger. You have all power to save in this world; but more importantly, You have the power to save above and beyond this world. I trust that You give life that lasts forever through Your Son, my Savior, Jesus Christ. Amen.

Repay the Right Way, Part 1

READ 1 PETER 3:8–22

KEY VERSES:

Keep your conscience clear. Then if people speak against you, they will be ashamed when they see what a good life you live because you belong to Christ. Remember, it is better to suffer for doing good, if that is what God wants, than to suffer for doing wrong!

1 PETER 3:16–17 NLT

UNDERSTAND:

- *In what ways do you search for peace and work to maintain it?*

- *How does suffering for what is right draw you into closer relationship with Jesus? Have you experienced this?*

APPLY:

If you've ever been insulted or spoken against unfairly, you know the instant urge to retaliate. It's in our sinful human nature to want to pay someone back for the hurtful thing they said. If you find yourself struggling with those frustrating feelings tonight—wanting to get revenge yet knowing you shouldn't, yet *really* wanting to anyway—let this scripture in 1 Peter 3 help settle your heart and mind. It certainly is a struggle to maintain self-control, especially in a situation where you are clearly in the right and the other party is clearly in the wrong. So maybe you need to put verse 9 on repeat in your mind: "Don't repay evil for evil. Don't retaliate with insults when people insult you. Instead, pay them back with a blessing. That is what God has called you to do, and he will grant you his blessing." As difficult as it is sometimes, choose to obey this scripture. It doesn't mean you are a doormat anyone can walk all over; it means you are a faithful child of God, and you choose to believe His promises. He is perfectly just and good, and we humans are not. Let Him handle the one who has wronged you, and let Him bless you as you choose to obey.

PRAY:

Heavenly Father, I am angry tonight, but I give this awful situation over to You. Please take away my anger and replace it with Your peace. Please help me to trust with patience that You will handle the situation in which I have been wronged. Show me how You want me to repay mistreatment with a blessing, and please shower me in return with Your blessing for being obedient. Thank You! Amen.

Repay the Right Way, Part 2

READ ROMANS 12

KEY VERSES:

Never pay back evil with more evil. Do things in such a way that everyone can see you are honorable. Do all that you can to live in peace with everyone.
ROMANS 12:17–18 NLT

UNDERSTAND:

- *What does it mean to heap burning coals on someone's head in the context of Romans 12?*

- *Have you ever felt conquered or nearly conquered by evil? What are ways you have conquered evil by doing good?*

APPLY:

It's not a one-and-done kind of lesson learned to "repay the right way." It's a struggle we'll probably all deal with time and again in life. Romans 12 offers instruction and encouragement on this topic too, especially verses 14–19. Like 1 Peter 3 tells us, it's clear we are urged to bless those who mistreat us and to let God handle justice. Then if you search the scriptures for more on this topic, you'll find in Matthew 5:44 that Jesus told us to love our enemies and pray for those who persecute us. And in Luke 6:27–37, Jesus taught more specifically about loving enemies, promising that when you do, "your reward from heaven will be very great, and you will truly be acting as children of the Most High." And what a priceless, unmerited treasure it is to be a child of the Most High! Remember that is truly who you are as you seek to honor God by obeying Him even when it seems so difficult to do.

PRAY:

Heavenly Father, I want to obey You regarding my enemies. I want to bless them, no matter how hard that is. Please forgive me when I have not; and going forward, please help me to let You be the one to make things right. Amen.

The Lord Has Chosen You

READ 1 CHRONICLES 28

KEY VERSE:

"Be strong and courageous, and do the work. Don't be afraid or discouraged, for the LORD God, my God, is with you. He will not fail you or forsake you."

1 CHRONICLES 28:20 NLT

UNDERSTAND:

- *What ways have you seen God help you determine what His plans are for you, rather than your own plans or someone else's plans for you?*

- *What work in your life do you feel you need extra strength and courage for right now?*

APPLY:

In this passage, King David assured his son Solomon that God had chosen him specifically to build the temple. He said in verse 10, "Take this seriously. The Lord has chosen you to build a Temple as his sanctuary. Be strong, and do the work." Do you believe God has specific plans and purposes for your life and that He chose you for specific tasks? Because He absolutely does and He has—even if sometimes you might feel like there is no way it's true or that you simply have no clue what that means. You can apply what David said to Solomon to your own life and reinforce it with the truth in Ephesians 2:10, which promises you are God's masterpiece, created new in Jesus to do the good things He planned for you long ago! When you're feeling lost and uninformed of those plans, you can find the map and itinerary in 1 Chronicles 28:9: "Learn to know the God of your ancestors intimately. Worship and serve him with your whole heart and a willing mind. For the Lord sees every heart and knows every plan and thought. If you seek him, you will find him. But if you forsake him, he will reject you forever."

PRAY:

Heavenly Father, I believe You have the best purposes and plans for my life. To know them, I simply need to keep striving to know You better and better, more and more. I choose to follow You, worship You, and seek You each and every day. When I get off track, please forgive me and quickly guide me back to You and Your will for my life. Amen.

Praise Be to God

READ PSALMS 66–67

KEY VERSES:

"All the earth bows down to you; they sing praise to you, they sing the praises of your name." Come and see what God has done, his awesome deeds for mankind!

Psalm 66:4–5 NIV

UNDERSTAND:

- *How has God tested and refined you like silver?*

- *Whom have you shared with lately about the good things God is doing in your life?*

APPLY:

When you head to bed after an awesome day full of goodness and blessing, praise God and thank Him! Let Psalms 66 and 67 inspire your words of gratitude. The anonymous writer of these psalms was clearly celebrating answered prayer. And don't miss a huge key to that answered prayer in Psalm 66:18–20: "If I had cherished sin in my heart, the Lord would not have listened; but God has surely listened and has heard my prayer. Praise be to God, who has not rejected my prayer or withheld his love from me!" As you celebrate blessings and answered prayer, think back to what sin you have avoided or recently confessed. Remember that God loves to listen to and reward those who faithfully obey Him, but He will turn His ear away from and withhold answers and blessing from those who cherish sin.

PRAY:

Heavenly Father, thank You for the many precious ways that You have listened to me and blessed me! Please always be so gracious to me, and shine Your face on me. Help me to never cherish sin but rather confess it to You. I will praise You and help proclaim You and Your goodness to all people! Amen.

When You Feel Weak and Helpless

READ JUDGES 6–7

KEY VERSE:

The LORD turned to [Gideon] and said, "Go with the strength you have, and rescue Israel from the Midianites. I am sending you!"
JUDGES 6:14 NLT

UNDERSTAND:

- *Gideon questioned God and told Him he felt abandoned by God. How did God respond to Gideon?*

- *Can you relate to feeling abandoned by God and questioning Him? If so, how has God responded to you?*

- *Have you ever asked God for a sign like Gideon did? Do you think Christians today should do that? When and why? Or why not?*

APPLY:

Despite his reservations, Gideon eventually obeyed and let God use him to lead in the defeat of a powerful enemy. Through God's great power, Gideon and an army that had dwindled to only three hundred men rescued Israel from the Midianites. Are you in a situation where you wish you could jump in and come to someone's rescue? Yet you feel helpless with no heroic qualities—and maybe you even feel like the weakest and worst, just like Gideon did? But the angel of the Lord had called Gideon a mighty hero because the Lord was with him, making him the hero. According to His will, God can use you in mighty and heroic ways if you simply obey and open yourself to letting Him do His good work through you.

PRAY:

Heavenly Father, I want to be available to You for any task, no matter how big or small, heroic or ordinary. Show me how You want me to serve You and others. Any good thing I am capable of and any good work I do are all because of Your love and power working through me. My life is from You and for You, Lord. I love and trust You! Amen.

God Knows What You Need

READ MATTHEW 6:25–34; LUKE 12:22–34

KEY VERSE:

"Look at the birds of the air; they do not sow or reap or store away in barns, and yet your heavenly Father feeds them. Are you not much more valuable than they?"

Matthew 6:26 NIV

UNDERSTAND:

- *What similarities and differences do you find in the two passages?*

- *What do you find yourself worrying about lately? How do these passages speak to those worries?*

APPLY:

What will we eat, what will we drink, what will we wear? Do you relate sometimes to the tone of that rather frantic series of questions? Maybe it's not literally food, beverage, and clothing that fill your mind with concerns right now, but the general idea could be the same. Most of our worries boil down to taking care of ourselves and our loved ones, both now and in the future. The higher our expectations and standard of living, the greater those worries might be because we'll have more to lose the more we expect and possess. So, we are wise to live as modestly as possible and hold gratefully and loosely to extra blessings beyond our most basic provisions. When we picture the refreshing simplicity of birds and flowers given beautiful purpose and being perfectly provided for, seemingly without a care in the world, we can be inspired to solely trust our Creator like they do. We are created in His image and are far more cherished and valued by Him. When we seek to know and love Him above everything else, we realize how everything we have is ultimately a gift from Him. He will never stop loving and caring and providing for us here on earth, and He is keeping all the very best gifts and treasures for us to enjoy perfectly forever in heaven.

PRAY:

Heavenly Father, again and again I need to release my worries about my needs and the needs of my loved ones to You. No one sees and cares and provides as well as You do. Please help me remember to trust that. Thank You for all You have already provided for me. Help me to realize how so much of what I have is extra blessing on top, and help me to strive to be as generous to others as You are to me. Amen.

Perfect Harmony

READ COLOSSIANS 3:1–17

KEY VERSES:

Put on then, as God's chosen ones, holy and beloved, compassionate hearts, kindness, humility, meekness, and patience, bearing with one another and, if one has a complaint against another, forgiving each other; as the Lord has forgiven you, so you also must forgive. And above all these put on love, which binds everything together in perfect harmony. And let the peace of Christ rule in your hearts.

Colossians 3:12–15 esv

UNDERSTAND:

- *Does the Word of Christ dwell in you richly?*

- *What is an example of setting your mind on things above instead of things of earth?*

- *What does it mean to do everything in the name of Jesus?*

APPLY:

Our days can be full of conflicts—little ones and big ones, with family members or friends, coworkers or managers, strangers at the store or in traffic. On a really bad day, maybe you've had conflict with all of them. Sometimes we handle conflicts well, and sometimes we don't. As you reflect on your day, you might smile with satisfaction over how you controlled your tongue in one setting but cringe at how you overreacted in another. Or you might still be holding on to lots of anger and frustration. Whatever the case, give it to God, and remember that His grace covers you. Ask Him to reveal your sin and show you where you need to forgive and to seek forgiveness. Let Him help you communicate well. Don't run from all conflict or difficult conversations tomorrow, but as you face them, remember that you are one of God's chosen. You can demonstrate a compassionate heart, kindness, meekness, and patience. You can give grace and forgiveness to others because you know how much grace and forgiveness God gives to you. Let His love bind everything together, and let His peace rule in your heart.

PRAY:

Heavenly Father, please focus my mind on heavenly things not the things of earth. Help me to rid my life of sin and fill it up with all the good things of You. I am one of Your chosen. I want to represent Your love and peace to others in everything I do. Amen.

Place of Safety

READ PSALM 18

KEY VERSES:

I love you, Lord; you are my strength. The Lord is my rock, my fortress, and my savior; my God is my rock, in whom I find protection. He is my shield, the power that saves me, and my place of safety.

Psalm 18:1–2 NLT

UNDERSTAND:

- *How have you seen God rescue in powerful and dramatic ways?*

- *How have you seen God rescue in quiet and subtle, yet strong and stable ways?*

- *Do you believe and sense that God delights in you?*

APPLY:

Too often we think and say that we truly believe God is our strength, but then we find ourselves trying to rely on our own strength instead. For sure, our own strength will fail us. Sometimes God wants that to happen in our lives so we remember that we need to lean and depend on Him, not ourselves. Let David's praise song in Psalm 18 remind you where you get true strength and stability and safety—from God alone. Remember awful moments when you felt afraid and in great danger, but then your heavenly Father protected and delivered you. Think of the details He orchestrated and people through whom He worked to help you. Picture and describe Him like David does as a fierce warrior coming to your rescue. Trust that God delights in you and rewards you for following His good ways. He loves to be faithful to those who are faithful to Him. Worship and praise Him for all these things every day, especially in ways that might make others want to love and trust Him too.

PRAY:

Heavenly Father, I love You, and You are my strength. You are my rock, my fortress, my Savior, and my shield. You are my power and my place of safety. If ever I am relying too much on myself, please draw me back to total dependence on You. Amen.

Answers in Unassuming Ways

READ 2 KINGS 5

KEY VERSES:

Now Naaman was commander of the army of the king of Aram. He was a great man in the sight of his master and highly regarded, because through him the Lord had given victory to Aram. He was a valiant soldier, but he had leprosy. Now bands of raiders from Aram had gone out and had taken captive a young girl from Israel, and she served Naaman's wife. She said to her mistress, "If only my master would see the prophet who is in Samaria! He would cure him of his leprosy." Naaman went to his master and told him what the girl from Israel had said. "By all means, go," the king of Aram replied.

2 Kings 5:1–5 NIV

UNDERSTAND:

- *Has God ever spoken to or led you in a totally unexpected, unassuming way?*

- *Who are the children in your life? How do they speak into your life and encourage you?*

APPLY:

Sometimes when we're praying for great needs, we hope for bold and impressive provision and guidance from God. Yet He often speaks to us and leads us in the most unassuming ways. This was the case for Naaman, who was a valiant army commander, highly respected by his master, the king of Aram. Yet he was obviously a humble man too and was willing to listen to a mere servant girl from Israel who had been taken captive and given to Naaman's wife. The young girl's advice—to go to Elisha, the prophet of the God of Israel, for healing from leprosy—was solid. Naaman was soon healed, and he gave God all the glory. We too should be humble like Naaman when we seek answers from God. Never be unwilling to listen to even the meekest, most modest among us if they are pointing us to more faith and dependence on God and His perfect Word.

PRAY:

Heavenly Father, I want to listen for You and sense Your direction and provision through any kind of circumstance or any person, whether impressive or modest. Please always keep me humble and teachable. Amen.

A Harvest of Righteousness and Peace

READ HEBREWS 12

KEY VERSE:

No discipline seems pleasant at the time, but painful. Later on, however, it produces a harvest of righteousness and peace for those who have been trained by it.

Hebrews 12:11 niv

UNDERSTAND:

- *How has discipline produced a good harvest in your life?*

- *What does it mean that "God is a consuming fire" in the final verse of Hebrews 12?*

APPLY:

The word *discipline* doesn't always bring peaceful thoughts to mind. We might think of angry arguments and punishments of the growing-up years and other kinds of consequences during rebellious times in our lives. But Hebrews 12 shows us how we *can* view discipline with peace—by realizing the hardship we endure is the discipline from God that is good for us in a loving, fatherly way. If we let Him, He strengthens us and proves our faith this way—just like good parents shouldn't always rescue their children from every hard thing. Rather, they let them experience difficulty and consequences so that they can develop strength and confidence in their own capabilities, plus learn from their mistakes. Once we have grown up, we appreciate the discipline good parents gave us as we develop into mature adults who contribute well to the world around us. Likewise, once we have reached the other side of a particular hardship, we can see how God used it in our lives to develop us plus produce "a harvest of righteousness and peace" that contributes to His kingdom.

PRAY:

Heavenly Father, please help me to focus on hardship in a positive way as good discipline from You. Teach me, strengthen me, and develop me in the midst of it, and give me peace that You are working it all for good. Amen.

Persistent Prayer

READ MATTHEW 7:7–11; LUKE 18:1–8; JOHN 15:7; EPHESIANS 6:18; 1 THESSALONIANS 5:17

KEY VERSE:

Jesus told his disciples a parable to show them that they should always pray and not give up.

LUKE 18:1 NIV

UNDERSTAND:

- *What is your current prayer life like? How could it improve?*

- *What is a prayer request you've had in the past that you are so thankful God didn't answer the way you originally hoped He would? How does what you've learned through that experience help you as you pray now?*

APPLY:

We all get tired of listening sometimes. We are human, and our listening ears wear out and lose patience. But God's listening ear never, ever fails. He never tires of hearing your prayers and requests. In fact, He urges you to keep them coming. No one else longs to hear from you like your heavenly Father does. He loves you like no person possibly can. He delights in giving you good gifts so much more than even the most loving parent does. And while He might not always answer your prayers *exactly* the way you had hoped, He will draw you into closer relationship with Him the more you talk to and listen to Him. And the closer you are to Him, the more you will realize the goodness of what He wants and your requests will better match His will.

PRAY:

Heavenly Father, I'm so grateful You never tire of hearing from me. I want to constantly improve my prayer time and relationship with You. Please keep drawing me closer to You, and match my will and wants with Yours. Amen.

READ 1 SAMUEL 1

KEY VERSES:

Hannah was in deep anguish, crying bitterly as she prayed to the Lord. And she made this vow: "O Lord of Heaven's Armies, if you will look upon my sorrow and answer my prayer and give me a son, then I will give him back to you. He will be yours for his entire lifetime, and as a sign that he has been dedicated to the Lord, his hair will never be cut."

1 Samuel 1:10–11 NLT

UNDERSTAND:

- *What was Eli's first response as he observed Hannah praying? Have you ever experienced something like that? How did that make you feel?*

- *How do you think Hannah must have felt as she followed through on her promise and took Samuel to the temple to live at such a young age? What does that say about her and her faith?*

APPLY:

Hannah knew what it felt like to think maybe God had forgotten or didn't care about her. Can you relate? Maybe you too are desperately praying for children right now, and God has not answered that desire. Or maybe you've been asking God to answer other requests to no avail. Whatever the case, don't give up. Let Hannah's story inspire you and give you peace tonight. She continued to pray for a son, and she showed her love and devotion to God by promising that if He agreed, she would let that son live at the temple to serve God his whole life. When God finally answered and blessed her with Samuel, Hannah followed through on her promise and was rewarded even more for her faithfulness. And Samuel grew to be a great prophet for God. He was a blessing to all the people of Israel because of Hannah's faithful prayer and promise.

PRAY:

Heavenly Father, please hear my requests and desires. Please help them to match Your perfect will for me. I promise to use my blessings to give back to You! Please help me to always keep that promise. Amen.

Give Your Burdens to the Lord

READ PSALMS 55–56

KEY VERSES:

When I am afraid, I will put my trust in you. I praise God for what he has promised. I trust in God, so why should I be afraid?

Psalm 56:3–4 NLT

UNDERSTAND:

- *What causes you to panic sometimes? How has God shown you He sees and cares?*

- *Have you ever been totally betrayed by someone you were once close to? What did God teach you through that experience?*

APPLY:

David's panicky words in Psalm 55:4–6 are sometimes oddly comforting in a misery-loves-company kind of way. He says, "My heart pounds in my chest. The terror of death assaults me. Fear and trembling overwhelm me, and I can't stop shaking. Oh, that I had wings like a dove; then I would fly away and rest!" We feel awful for David, yet if we've experienced any kind of horrible upset, we can probably relate. And it's good to know we're not the only ones who've ever felt that way—terrified with a racing heart and wishing we could just fly away quickly to find peace and rest. Like David, we can vent our feelings of total fear and frustration to God. We can tell our heavenly Father about our panic and pain. No one understands and cares like He does. As we cry out, we must hold on to the promise that our good Father sees every one of our sorrows. If we trust in Him, He will guide us to and send us the help we need. He rescues us, defends us against our enemies, and helps us walk confidently in His life-giving light.

PRAY:

Heavenly Father, I relate to David in his panic sometimes. Please calm me with the truth of Your promises. Please send me the help and encouragement I need. Please guide and direct me through Your people, provision, and perfect peace. I trust You, and I love You! Amen.

The Lord Is with You, So Don't Be Afraid

READ NUMBERS 13:1–14:12

KEY VERSES:

If the LORD is pleased with us, he will bring us safely into that land and give it to us. It is a rich land flowing with milk and honey. Do not rebel against the LORD, and don't be afraid of the people of the land. They are only helpless prey to us! They have no protection, but the LORD is with us! Don't be afraid of them!"

NUMBERS 14:8–9 NLT

UNDERSTAND:

- *Do you ever struggle with complaining to God about your circumstances or what He has asked you to do? How does the account of the twelve spies in Canaan help you correct that?*

- *Have you experienced a time when you listened to fear rather than let God make you confident and brave? Or do you celebrate a time when you were tempted to give in to fear but were motivated by God's promises instead? What did you learn?*

APPLY:

Obeying God's direction, Moses sent out men to explore the land of Canaan because God had said to Moses that He was one day soon going to give it to His people, the Israelites. So, Joshua, Caleb, and ten other men went to spy on the land of Canaan for forty days. When they returned, they reported that the land was wonderful, flowing with milk and honey and all kinds of bounty. However, the people of Canaan were very powerful, and the cities were well protected. Joshua and Caleb weren't intimidated though. They were confident that with God's help they could still take over Canaan. But the ten other spies adamantly opposed because of their fear. The ten spread fear so well among the Israelites that they rebelled and complained against Moses and Aaron. God grew angry with the Israelites because they listened to fear rather than listening to the courage and faith of Joshua and Caleb. So, He punished the majority of the people but blessed Joshua and Caleb.

PRAY:

Heavenly Father, like Joshua and Caleb, I know You are with me, and I don't need to be afraid of what might seem too hard for me to handle. I have Your power and strength with me at all times. I want to choose faith over fear, no matter what I am facing. Please embolden and bless me according to Your will. Amen.

Simplify

READ MATTHEW 25:31–46

KEY VERSE:

"The King will reply, 'Truly I tell you, whatever you did for one of the least of these brothers and sisters of mine, you did for me.' "

MATTHEW 25:40 NIV

UNDERSTAND:

- *What areas of life or relationships cause you the most concern about whether you are doing a good job or doing enough?*

- *How has your relationship with Jesus grown as you care for others in need?*

APPLY:

As women, we so often worry about whether or not we are doing enough, doing the right things, and doing them well—in our marriages, our parenting, our friendships, our homes, our jobs, our ministry, and so on. Sometimes we need to simplify and stop trying so hard. We need to ask God to help us focus on the good things He planned for us to do when He created us. We should ask Him to show us the relationships He wants us to invest in the most, starting with Him. And this scripture in Matthew should remind us that the very best job anyone can have is to serve our King by serving others. We are always doing the right thing if we are doing even the simplest act of kindness for someone in need. There is such peace and contentment when we realize how rewarding it is to care for others as if caring for Jesus Himself—because truly we are.

PRAY:

Loving Savior, please remind me how my service and care for others in need is truly service and care for You. With every good thing I do to help someone else, I grow closer to You. Thank You for such wonderful purpose in my life. Please help me to simplify my life and focus on the good things You have planned for me to do. Amen.

A Second Chance

READ JONAH 1–3

KEY VERSES:

Then the LORD spoke to Jonah a second time: "Get up and go to the great city of Nineveh, and deliver the message I have given you." This time Jonah obeyed the LORD's command and went to Nineveh, a city so large that it took three days to see it all.

JONAH 3:1–3 NLT

UNDERSTAND:

- *Have you ever had a Jonah type of experience in your life?*

- *How have second chances from God helped you develop more faith and gratitude?*

APPLY:

Jonah is a great story to revisit when you feel like you've been called by God to a place or situation you don't really want to be in. Just like Jonah, you might be tempted to go in "the opposite direction to get away from the LORD" (Jonah 1:3 NLT). That's what Jonah did, and the consequences are an unforgettable lesson. None of us wants to end up in the belly of a whale, literally or figuratively, for disobeying God. But the best part of the lesson is remembering God's great love and gracious mercy toward us, evidenced especially in Jonah's prayer in Jonah 2:2: "I cried out to the LORD in my great trouble, and he answered me. I called to you from the land of the dead, and LORD, you heard me!" Our holy God had every right to ignore Jonah for his disobedience, but instead He listened. He loved Jonah and had mercy on him, and you can feel Jonah's gratitude and praise in the words of his prayer. God gave Jonah a second chance, and the story reminds us that God loves to give us second chances as well.

PRAY:

Heavenly Father, help me to remember Jonah when I'm feeling like I don't want to obey. Remind me of the lessons he learned. Thank You for Your grace and mercy to give me many second chances as well. Amen.

Beautiful Beatitudes

READ MATTHEW 5:1–20

KEY VERSES:

"God blesses you when people mock you and persecute you and lie about you and say all sorts of evil things against you because you are my followers. Be happy about it! Be very glad! For a great reward awaits you in heaven."

MATTHEW 5:11–12 NLT

UNDERSTAND:

- *Do you feel truly glad when you suffer for following Jesus? If not, how can you work on changing your attitude about this?*

- *What ways do you try to shine your light for Jesus for all to see?*

APPLY:

Did you know the word *beatitude* means "state of utmost bliss"? What a lovely definition to think of as you read Jesus' Sermon on the Mount and His famous Beatitudes. His teaching here turns most everything that is glamorized in today's popular culture completely upside down. The world doesn't generally glamorize feeling poor and in need of God. Nor does it glamorize mourning, humility, or a hunger for what is right and true. The world also doesn't glamorize being full of mercy, having a pure heart, working for peace, or being persecuted and mocked for doing what is right and following Jesus. Yet Jesus did glamorize and idealize all these things as He promised great blessings and rewards for those who experienced them. As we live out our faith in Him, trusting in the incredible promises of the Beatitudes, we become the salt and light of the earth. We become what the world around us needs to taste and see about God so that they will trust in Jesus as their Savior too.

PRAY:

Dear Jesus, help me to remember Your beautiful teaching in the Sermon on the Mount. I trust in Your salvation and blessings. Help me to display Your dramatic difference in this world, which will point others to wanting to know and love and serve You too. Amen.

Faithful Friendship

READ RUTH 1

KEY VERSES:

Ruth replied, "Don't ask me to leave you and turn back. Wherever you go, I will go; wherever you live, I will live. Your people will be my people, and your God will be my God. Wherever you die, I will die, and there I will be buried. May the LORD punish me severely if I allow anything but death to separate us!"

RUTH 1:16–17 NLT

UNDERSTAND:

- *Orpah was conflicted at first, but then she decided to leave Naomi. What motivated Ruth's fierce loyalty to Naomi instead of choosing to go with Orpah?*

- *Have you ever felt as low as Naomi as described in Ruth 1:20–21? How did God lift you up?*

APPLY:

Every woman needs such a loyal woman in her life as Ruth was to Naomi. If you have that kind of faithful friend or relative, praise God for her and make sure she knows how grateful you are for her. Nurture that relationship. If you have more than one woman in your life like that, you are extremely blessed! And if you need a faithful friend, pray for God to help you make the connection. He knows and cares that you need good friendship, and He will help you find it. His Word says, "Two people are better off than one, for they can help each other succeed. If one person falls, the other can reach out and help. But someone who falls alone is in real trouble. Likewise, two people lying close together can keep each other warm. But how can one be warm alone? A person standing alone can be attacked and defeated, but two can stand back-to-back and conquer. Three are even better, for a triple-braided cord is not easily broken" (Ecclesiastes 4:9–12 NLT).

PRAY:

Heavenly Father, thank You for the gift of loyal friendship. Please bless my friends, and help us grow in our relationships with each other and with You! Amen.

God Is Always the Same

READ PSALM 102; MALACHI 3:6;
HEBREWS 13:8; JAMES 1:17

KEY VERSES:

You made the earth in the beginning. You made the heavens with Your hands. They will be destroyed but You will always live. They will all become old as clothing becomes old. You will change them like a coat. And they will be changed, but You are always the same. Your years will never end.

Psalm 102:25–27 NLV

UNDERSTAND:

- *What are the ways you enjoy change, and what are the things you wish would always stay the same?*

- *What changes cause you the most stress?*

- *In addition to Psalm 102, how do the scriptures in Malachi 3:6, Hebrews 13:8, and James 1:17 give you peace, knowing that God is unchanging?*

APPLY:

Life is always changing. Some of us thrive on that and some of us don't. We all have some things we love to change and other things we wish would always stay the same. No matter what changes we experience in our circumstances, relationships, and the world around us, it's so good to know that God is our one true constant. He is steady and strong and eternally true, and we can put all our faith in Him. We can build our lives on Him. We can trust that He is the perfect Creator with perfect plans, and He is sovereign over all places and times forever. That truth should fill us with a steady, strong peace that prevails throughout our lives.

PRAY:

Heavenly Father, thank You for being the same yesterday, today, and forever. I need Your steady, unchanging presence and love every moment of my life. I need to remember that You always have been and always will be, and Your perfect plans for all of creation will prevail no matter what. Amen.

The Right People, Places, and Details

READ JOSHUA 2

KEY VERSES:

The king of Jericho sent to Rahab, saying, "Bring out the men who have come to you, who entered your house, for they have come to search out all the land." But the woman had taken the two men and hidden them.

JOSHUA 2:3–4 ESV

UNDERSTAND:

- *Have you experienced a time when you could clearly see God's hand through the people He made available to you exactly when you needed them?*

- *What tiny details have you seen God's hand in as He helps and directs you?*

APPLY:

The two men Joshua sent to spy on the land of Canaan had to be anxious about their mission. Hopefully, you're not facing anything quite so dangerous as they did; but whatever stressful thing might be weighing heavily on you tonight, let the story be an encouragement to you. God provides the right people in the right places to help you in your troubles, just like He provided Rahab to help hide and protect the two spies in her home. She told them that she trusted in their God. In turn, the spies promised to help protect Rahab and her family as long as she did not tell anyone about their plans. Then Rahab lowered them by a rope through the window and urged them to hide for three days in the hill country before returning home. Later, with that same red rope, the spies knew where to find her and her family to protect them from being killed when the Israelites took over Jericho.

PRAY:

Heavenly Father, thank You for the way You orchestrate exactly the right people in exactly the right places with exactly the right details to help those who love and follow You. I trust that You do that for me, and I'm so grateful. Amen.

You Do You

READ 1 CORINTHIANS 12

KEY VERSES:

God works in different ways, but it is the same God who does the work in all of us. A spiritual gift is given to each of us so we can help each other.

1 CORINTHIANS 12:6–7 NLT

UNDERSTAND:

- *How has God shown you what your gifts, talents, and abilities are?*

- *Do you sometimes wish you had more or different gifts instead?*

- *How are you using your gifts to strengthen the body of believers and serve God and others?*

APPLY:

Too often, we compare ourselves to others and wish we could be like them. If you find yourself doing that, let 1 Corinthians 12 refresh you. You have been given the specific gifts, talents, and personality you have on purpose by God through His Holy Spirit. He has plans and purposes that are unique for you. You are not supposed to be exactly like anyone else because God wants you to do you. By incredible design, God will work what His plans are for you in coordination with what His plans are for others to create unity, love, and care among believers. When the Church does this as God intends, it is the best way to display the great love He has for us and help others want to become believers as well.

PRAY:

Heavenly Father, please remind me that my gifts are unique. I want to use what You have given me enthusiastically for You, doing my special part in the body of believers. Help me not to compare or become dissatisfied or envious. I am grateful to serve You and demonstrate Your love. Amen.

At All Times

READ PSALM 34

KEY VERSES:

I will bless the LORD at all times; his praise shall continually be in my mouth. My soul makes its boast in the LORD; let the humble hear and be glad. Oh, magnify the LORD with me, and let us exalt his name together!

PSALM 34:1–3 ESV

UNDERSTAND:

- *How much time do you spend in worship and prayer each day?*

- *What do you think might change in your life if you increased your worship and prayer time?*

APPLY:

We can alleviate so much of our stress and worries if we make the first few verses of Psalm 34 true of ourselves. If we bless and praise God at all times, boast in His amazing goodness and power, and lift up His name for others to know and honor Him, we don't have much time to focus on problems and pain. Our minds will stay fixed on the one who encamps around us, the one who hears and delivers us from every fear. Name anything you are anxious over, hurting from, or frightened about tonight, and speak praise to God over and above it. Tell God you know that He sees and cares about every detail of the situation and that He is sovereign and good through it all. Describe to Him how you see that He has been caring for you in the midst of it, and trust that He will continue to do so. Breathe deeply as you pray and worship, letting God's peace quiet you and give you rest.

PRAY:

Heavenly Father, You are awesome and mighty in all things. I choose to fix my thoughts and words on You in worship for all that You are and all the good that You do! Please push out every problem and pain from my mind as I praise You! Amen.

The Lord's Battle

READ 1 SAMUEL 17:32–51

KEY VERSES:

"Don't worry about this Philistine," David told Saul. "I'll go fight him!" "Don't be ridiculous!" Saul replied. "There's no way you can fight this Philistine and possibly win! You're only a boy, and he's been a man of war since his youth." But David persisted. . . . The Lord who rescued me from the claws of the lion and the bear will rescue me from this Philistine!"

1 Samuel 17:32–37 NLT

UNDERSTAND:

- *What stood out as most familiar to you about the story of David and Goliath? What stood out as something you'd never heard of or thought much about before?*

- *Saul tried to equip David with heavy sword and armor, but instead David just wanted his regular clothes and humble weapon. What does that say about David's character and faith? How does that inspire you?*

APPLY:

Another classic Bible story is the one of David and Goliath, and maybe we need the reminder tonight that no giant is too big for God to defeat. We should remember the scene in verses 41 through 46 as we face any kind of foe or difficulty. The current "Goliath" in our lives—whether a person or situation or whether physical, spiritual, mental, or all of the above—might be sneering and cursing at us, saying things like, "Am I a dog. . .that you come at me with a stick? . . . Come over here, and I'll give your flesh to the birds and wild animals!" But we can respond with courageous confidence like David: "You come to me with sword, spear, and javelin, but I come to you in the name of the LORD of Heaven's Armies—the God of the armies of Israel, whom you have defied. Today the LORD will conquer you!" We should picture that scene and then Goliath's defeat as we face our battles; ultimately, they are the Lord's. It doesn't matter how big our enemy or what its worldly weapons are. We have the Lord of heaven's armies on our side. The critical key is to take no pride in our own power and give no credit to ourselves. Simply let God work in and around us. David knew—and we do too—that his strength and ability to defeat his enemy were given by God, and it was for His glory and to spread His great renown.

PRAY:

Heavenly Father, in Your great name and in Your mighty power, I can stand up to any enemy and fight in any battle. Because of You, no one can defeat me. I trust You, my Almighty God and loving Savior! Amen.

Experience God's Peace

READ PHILIPPIANS 4

KEY VERSES:

Don't worry about anything; instead, pray about everything. Tell God what you need, and thank him for all he has done. Then you will experience God's peace, which exceeds anything we can understand. His peace will guard your hearts and minds as you live in Christ Jesus.

PHILIPPIANS 4:6–7 NLT

UNDERSTAND:

- *Do you have any disagreements with other women, like Euodia and Syntyche did, in your life right now that you need to resolve and reconcile?*

- *Do you do well in thinking about things that are true, honorable, right, pure, lovely, admirable, excellent, and worthy of praise? How can you be constantly growing and improving in this (verse 8)?*

APPLY:

God's Word promises that if we pray rather than worry about everything, telling God what we need and thanking Him for what He has done, we will experience God's peace beyond all our understanding. It doesn't say God will instantly fix our problems or immediately give us whatever we ask for, but it promises inexplicable peace, the kind only God can give. Talking to God in prayer with gratitude demonstrates our trust in Him and love for Him. It reminds us of all He has done and is able to do. It fills us with confidence that He has sovereign power over all things, including every detail of our lives. We draw closer in relationship with our Father the more we talk to Him in prayer. The closer we are to the Father, the more we realize we need less of anything else and simply more of focusing on Him, who He is, and all He is able to do, to be in perfect peace.

PRAY:

Heavenly Father, remind me that every problem pales when I focus on You. I thank You for all You have done, and I trust You to provide all that I truly need. Please fill me with Your extraordinary peace. Amen.

God's Magnificent Creation

READ GENESIS 1:1–2:3

KEY VERSES:

So the heavens and the earth were completed, and all that is in them. On the seventh day God ended His work which He had done. And He rested on the seventh day from all His work which He had done.

Genesis 2:1–2 NLV

UNDERSTAND:

- *Why do you think the phrase "God saw that it was good" is repeated throughout Genesis 1?*

- *Why are people different from the rest of creation?*

APPLY:

Spending time outdoors in God's magnificent creation can surely help release any anxiety and fill you with peace. When you look at a beautiful sunset, when you go for a hike in a thick forest or on a majestic mountain trail, when you swim in a rippling lake, when you pick a gorgeous wild-flower, when you do anything that makes you focus on and appreciate nature, praise your amazing Creator God! The natural world He designed and gave us is truly extraordinary. It reminds us in countless ways how awesome He is. He planned and created land and air and sea and plants and animals with incredible love, detail, beauty, and purpose. And if He created all that so marvelously, how much more did He create you, who are created in His image, with incredible love, detail, beauty, and purpose? Rest well tonight, dreaming of creation and about how dearly loved you are by your Creator.

PRAY:

Heavenly Father, thank You for Your awesome creation. It reminds me every day how incredible You are and how dearly loved I am. I praise You and I love You! Amen.

God Leads the Way

READ ISAIAH 42

KEY VERSE:

"I will lead the blind by a way that they do not know. I will lead them in paths they do not know. I will turn darkness into light in front of them. And I will make the bad places smooth. These are the things I will do and I will not leave them."

Isaiah 42:16 NLV

UNDERSTAND:

- *Isaiah 42:6 says God will take hold of your hand. Are you doing your part by reaching out for Him and letting Him keep your hand in His?*

- *Do you regularly sing to the Lord a new song like verse 10 describes? How does that help fill you with peace?*

APPLY:

Have you ever tripped or stubbed your toe because you were fumbling around in the dark? You might feel as though that is how you are living your life—in total darkness. Maybe you just cannot see the right way to go when making a big decision or facing a big problem in your job or in your marriage and so on. So, trust this scripture, where God promises to turn darkness into light and make rocky places smooth for His people. He will open new paths for you when you don't know what to do or where to go, and He will never leave you! Keep praying and keep trusting!

PRAY:

Heavenly Father, I'm following You even when I cannot see where You are taking me. I trust You to take me on good paths and make all the rough spots smooth. Thank You for leading me and never leaving me. Amen.

Don't Let Your Heart Be Troubled

READ JOHN 14:1–27

KEY VERSE:

"I am leaving you with a gift—peace of mind and heart. And the peace I give is a gift the world cannot give. So don't be troubled or afraid."

JOHN 14:27 NLT

UNDERSTAND:

- *How does the promise of Jesus preparing a place for you in heaven help keep your heart from being troubled here on earth?*

- *Do you relate to Thomas, Philip, or Judas in this passage? Why?*

APPLY:

Some of Jesus' disciples were clearly confused here in this passage. That's kind of comforting, isn't it? These men had spent so much time with Jesus. They had sat under His teaching. They had seen Him perform miracles. Time and again He had proven for them to see that He is God, and yet they still doubted and questioned! That ought to give you comfort and peace when you are doubting and questioning too. Thomas, Philip, and Judas had spent time with Jesus in the flesh. Here we are, thousands of years past when our Savior lived and taught in person on the earth, and yet we hold on dearly to our faith in Him. So, if Jesus patiently, lovingly answered *their* questions, surely He has even more patience and love for *ours*. Maybe some nights you are praying questions like Thomas, Philip, and Judas asked. In those times, remember the answers Jesus gave: He is the way, the truth, and the life. He is God. He reveals Himself to those who seek after Him, obey Him, and love Him. He has sent the Holy Spirit to live in us and help us and remind us of everything He taught. And He offers peace that is out-of-this-world awesome!

PRAY:

Dear Jesus, thank You for Your patience and love for those who question and doubt like I do sometimes. Through Your Holy Spirit who is in me, remind me of all You have taught and promised. Please lead me and guide me in Your Word, reveal Yourself to me, and fill me with Your extraordinary peace. Amen.

The Very Best Promise Keeper

READ NUMBERS 23

KEY VERSE:

God is not human, that he should lie, not a human being, that he should change his mind. Does he speak and then not act? Does he promise and not fulfill?
Numbers 23:19 NIV

UNDERSTAND:

- *God can use anyone and anything to speak His message and truth. What ways have you experienced this?*

- *What promises have you seen God fulfill firsthand? How has that strengthened your faith?*

APPLY:

Even though Balaam was a wicked prophet, God still spoke truth through him—and the message Balaam spoke from God can help give us peace today when we focus on how God always keeps His promises. He will never let us down the way other people might. He is the only one who can make a perfect promise and always fulfill it. He is not human, and He cannot lie or make mistakes. When He speaks, His Word is always right and true. At times, the very best people who love us the most will let us down, even if they don't mean to, because they are human. But God is above and beyond us, and we can trust Him completely.

PRAY:

Heavenly Father, thank You for always being true and keeping Your Word! Help me to remember that You are so much better than any human being. You are our loving, incredible Creator and the very best promise keeper. Amen.

Let the Lord Refresh You

READ ISAIAH 58

KEY VERSE:

The Lord will always lead you. He will meet the needs of your soul in the dry times and give strength to your body. You will be like a garden that has enough water, like a well of water that never dries up.

Isaiah 58:11 NLV

UNDERSTAND:

- *What makes your soul feel dry at times? How do you let God refresh you?*

- *How do you apply verses 13–14 in your life?*

APPLY:

Do you have plants in your home that are near death because no one remembers to water them? They start to look pretty sad, don't they? Or think of your lawn or garden in the middle of a hot summer with no rain. Sometimes we start to feel dry and ugly like that in our souls when we aren't spending good time with God. We need to read His Word and pray and worship Him so that He can lead and refresh us. We also need to fellowship with other believers who regularly do these things. God gives the kind of living water that makes us never feel thirsty again. When Jesus spoke to the woman at the well, He meant it for us too: "Whoever drinks the water I give them will never thirst. Indeed, the water I give them will become in them a spring of water welling up to eternal life" (John 4:14 NIV).

PRAY:

Lord, please lead me. Meet the needs of my soul in dry times, and give strength to my soul. Thank You for refreshing me and restoring me with Your extraordinary living water! Amen.

One in Christ

READ GALATIANS 3

KEY VERSES:

You are now children of God because you have put your trust in Christ Jesus. All of you who have been baptized to show you belong to Christ have become like Christ. God does not see you as a Jew or as a Greek. He does not see you as a servant or as a person free to work. He does not see you as a man or as a woman. You are all one in Christ.

Galatians 3:26–28 NLV

UNDERSTAND:

- *Have you been baptized? Why or why not?*

- *Do you ever struggle with feeling "less than" when compared to others? How does this scripture encourage you?*

APPLY:

The word *equality* is thrown around a lot these days, and it's important to remember that only Jesus gives true equality. Because of sin in the world, people will never get equality exactly right. There will always be bad people trying to say some groups of people are better than others—but that's always a lie. In God's eyes, because of Jesus, every single person is the same in value. We all matter so much to God that He sent Jesus to die to save us from our sins. And when anyone trusts in Jesus, they become a child of the one true God, the King of all kings. That makes us all equally royal! The secular world will tell you all kinds of ways to help promote equality, some good and some bad, but most important of all is to spread the gospel of Jesus Christ, because in Him alone are we all truly equal.

PRAY:

Heavenly Father, thank You that anyone can be Your child by trusting that only Jesus saves. You offer the only true equality through Him. Help me to share the awesome truth of that with others in this sinful world. Amen.

Be Slow to Anger

READ PSALM 86; PROVERBS 14:29; 19:11; ECCLESIASTES 7:9; EPHESIANS 4:26; JAMES 1:19–21

KEY VERSE:

You, O Lord, are a God merciful and gracious, slow to anger and abounding in steadfast love and faithfulness.

Psalm 86:15 esv

UNDERSTAND:

- *What are the common triggers of your anger? Do you do well by dealing with angry feelings in healthy ways, or is this something you need to improve?*

- *How is anger good and helpful sometimes?*

APPLY:

Women often like to joke about how hormonal changes or lack of sleep or caffeine or food makes us crabby and quickly angry. Yet we need to be careful we don't make light of this too much. Since our righteous, merciful, gracious God is slow to anger with us, we should strive to be the same with others, no matter what time of the month or how little sleep or whether or not we've had our morning coffee and afternoon snacks. And yikes, it is hard to do! So, study the scriptures on the topic of anger, and let God instruct and correct you. Remember that not all anger is bad, and ask God to show you when it is good and just. Seek forgiveness from those who have received the brunt of your sinful anger, and then humbly admit how much you require God's help with understanding and controlling anger in healthy ways. We can humbly pray about this topic, as Psalm 86:1 begins: "Incline your ear, O Lord, and answer me, for I am poor and needy."

PRAY:

Heavenly Father, since You are slow to anger, I certainly should be too! I need Your help when I feel cranky. Help me not to angrily lash out at others. Help me to pause and pray, and please fill me with self-control and peace instead. Amen.

The Best Kind of Rest

READ MATTHEW 11

KEY VERSES:

"Come to me, all you who are weary and burdened, and I will give you rest. Take my yoke upon you and learn from me, for I am gentle and humble in heart, and you will find rest for your souls. For my yoke is easy and my burden is light."

MATTHEW 11:28–30 NIV

UNDERSTAND:

- *How do verses 4–6 help give you peace tonight?*

- *Do you feel weary and burdened lately? How are you seeking rest in Jesus?*

APPLY:

The best kind of rest is the kind Jesus gives. It's not like a great nap or a spa day or a perfect vacation. It's even better. It's a way of life that gives you deep peace because you ask Jesus to be your Savior, you follow Him, and you learn from Him. Yes, sometimes things in life are tiring and stressful. But turning to Jesus in those times reminds you to slow down and let Him take away the worries as you trust in Him. "Cast all your anxiety on him because he cares for you," 1 Peter 5:7 says. What an amazing Savior we have! We should constantly be saying, "Praise be to the Lord, to God our Savior, who daily bears our burdens" (Psalm 68:19 NIV).

PRAY:

Loving Savior, please help me to breathe deeply, slow down, and give You any worries and weariness I have. You give the best kind of rest as I follow You. Thank You for bearing my burdens every day! Amen.

Remember When

READ EXODUS 13

KEY VERSE:

Moses said to the people, "Remember this day in which you went out of Egypt, out of the land where you were made to stay and work. For the Lord brought you out of this place by a powerful hand."

Exodus 13:3 NLV

UNDERSTAND:

- *What events or circumstances in your life are hard but good for you to review as you see how God rescued you?*

- *God used a pillar of cloud by day and a pillar of fire by night to lead the Israelites in the wilderness. In what unique ways has He led you?*

APPLY:

We often want to forget the bad things we've experienced and endured, because they were awful and we're so glad they're over. We want our brains to block them completely. In some ways, though, it's good to remember them so that we never forget how God helped and rescued us. Looking back and remembering grows our faith and helps us trust that God will deliver us again in the future. Moses told the people of Israel to remember the amazing day that God finally brought them out of slavery in Egypt. In the same way, we should remember all the incredible ways God has helped and rescued us from difficulty and danger.

PRAY:

Heavenly Father, every bit of help and rescue I have ever received ultimately comes from You! I don't ever want to forget, and I trust You to help and rescue me again and again. I am so grateful! Amen.

Dream Home

READ PSALMS 84–85

KEY VERSES:

How beautiful are the places where You live, O Lord of all! My soul wants and even becomes weak from wanting to be in the house of the Lord. . . . How happy are those who live in Your house! They are always giving thanks to You.

Psalm 84:1–4 NLV

UNDERSTAND:

- *How have you experienced God as your sun and safe-covering as Psalm 84:11 describes?*

- *How does Psalm 84:12 help give you peace tonight?*

APPLY:

Do you have a dream home you like to imagine living in? It's fun to think about, even while we choose to be content and make our actual homes a restful and comfortable place in which to live. And every woman has different styles and tastes for her home. But better than anything we can dream up and create here on earth is the forever home God is creating for us in heaven. It will be incredible! When we take time to focus on God, praise Him, and hear from Him through His Word, we get little glimpses of how awesomely perfect our forever home will be!

PRAY:

Heavenly Father, thank You for my blessings here and now where I live on earth; but even more, thank You for the perfect forever home with You that You are making for me in heaven! Amen.

The One Who Lives in You

READ 1 JOHN 4

KEY VERSE:

My children, you are a part of God's family. You have stood against these false preachers and had power over them. You had power over them because the One Who lives in you is stronger than the one who is in the world.

1 John 4:4 NLV

UNDERSTAND:

- *What does this passage say is the test for knowing what is truly from the Spirit of God?*

- *How do verses 16–18 speak comfort to any anxieties in your life right now?*

APPLY:

"The One Who lives in you is stronger than the one who is in the world"—that last part of 1 John 4:4 is such a short and simple yet powerful scripture to memorize and repeat when you need strength and courage in any situation. Our enemy the devil is the one stirring up all kinds of evil in this world. And you will be under attack from him sometimes, in all sorts of different ways—through stressful times for your family, through painful times of loss, through illness, and so on. But no matter how strong the enemy and his evil seem against you and your loved ones, he is never stronger than the power of God in you through the Holy Spirit. Don't ever forget that. Call on Him to help you be strong, calm, and patient and to help you see how He is working and taking care of you through it all.

PRAY:

Heavenly Father, deep down I know You are always stronger than any evil attack against me, any hard thing I'm going through. But I do forget that truth sometimes, and I'm sorry. Please remind me, fill me with Your power and peace, and do the fighting for me. Amen.

Marriage Matters

READ 1 CORINTHIANS 13; HEBREWS 13:4–5; EPHESIANS 5:22–33; COLOSSIANS 3:18–25

KEY VERSE:

Love bears all things, believes all things, hopes all things, endures all things.

1 Corinthians 13:7 ESV

UNDERSTAND:

- *What is going well in your marriage right now that gives you great peace and joy?*

- *What are areas that might need work in your marriage?*

- *What struggles have you overcome in your marriage, and how does this give you hope and peace for present and future struggles?*

APPLY:

The love passage of 1 Corinthians 13 is so popular at weddings, and rightfully so. The basis for a great marriage should be the godly, sacrificial love it describes. If you are struggling with any marriage matters right now, both you and your husband need to sincerely evaluate the way you love each other in light of this passage and all the Bible says about godly love and marriage. It's easier said than done, of course, but prayer is where heart change can begin. Ask God to show you both where you need to adjust and improve. Communicate respectfully with each other first, and get outside godly wisdom and help if you need to. Pray faithfully and continually, even if you don't see answers and improvements right away. Ask for more and more grace, love, and wisdom. Celebrate progress and the things you naturally do well. Most of all, hold fast to your commitment and the sacredness of marriage, and let God bless you as you do.

PRAY:

Heavenly Father, please protect and bring great peace and joy to my marriage as my husband and I seek to honor You most of all with our commitment and relationship. Help us to love each other sacrificially and sacredly. Amen.

Make the Lord Your Refuge

READ PSALMS 91–92

KEY VERSES:

The L*ORD says, "I will rescue those who love me. I will protect those who trust in my name. When they call on me, I will answer; I will be with them in trouble. I will rescue and honor them. I will reward them with a long life and give them my salvation."*

PSALM 91:14–16 NLT

UNDERSTAND:

- *Psalm 91:2 tells us God alone should be our place of refuge. In what wrong places have you sought refuge in the past or have watched other people seek refuge? What did that teach you?*

- *When have you sensed God's angels protecting you?*

APPLY:

Whatever fears are tormenting you lately, let Psalms 91 and 92 quiet them tonight. Trust that as you put your hope in God alone as your refuge, He protects you from absolutely any danger or threat to your life. According to His will for your life here on earth, nothing can ever defeat you. More importantly, through His Son, Jesus Christ, He protects you eternally by giving you life that lasts forever in heaven with Him. Believe in His promises that He has ordered His angels to protect you wherever you go and that He listens to your cries for help and rescues you. Then, as Psalm 92 does, thank and praise God for all His care and protection. Thank and praise Him for the ways He shelters you while arming and strengthening you as He helps you flourish and thrive.

PRAY:

Heavenly Father, You are the Most High, and I am so grateful to live in Your shelter and find rest in Your shadow. Please quiet my fears with the truth of all Your promises. I proclaim Your love and faithfulness, and I exalt You, God! Amen.

Pleasant and Peaceful

READ PHILIPPIANS 2

KEY VERSES:

God is helping you obey Him. God is doing what He wants done in you. Be glad you can do the things you should be doing. Do all things without arguing and talking about how you wish you did not have to do them. In that way, you can prove yourselves to be without blame. You are God's children and no one can talk against you, even in a sin-loving and sin-sick world. You are to shine as lights among the sinful people of this world.

PHILIPPIANS 2:13–15 NLV

UNDERSTAND:

- *How does imitating Christ in His humility help fill you with peace?*

- *How does keeping a positive attitude, without grumbling or complaining, help fill you with peace?*

APPLY:

Yikes, it's terribly hard to do *all* things without ever arguing or complaining, isn't it? But that's what this scripture encourages us to do. It's something with which we all need a lot of help from God. But if we can keep positive with our words as we obey God and follow the plans He has for us, we shine as extra-bright lights in the dark and sinful world around us. Hopefully, people who do not trust Jesus as their Savior will want to know more about God's love because they will see our lights shining in our pleasant and peaceful attitudes, no matter the situation.

PRAY:

Heavenly Father, please help me to be extraordinary light in the darkness of sin around me in this world. I want to shine so brightly that others want to know Jesus as their Savior too. Amen.

The Vine and the Branches

READ JOHN 15

KEY VERSES:

"I am the true grapevine, and my Father is the gardener. He cuts off every branch of mine that doesn't produce fruit, and he prunes the branches that do bear fruit so they will produce even more. You have already been pruned and purified by the message I have given you. Remain in me, and I will remain in you. For a branch cannot produce fruit if it is severed from the vine, and you cannot be fruitful unless you remain in me. Yes, I am the vine; you are the branches. Those who remain in me, and I in them, will produce much fruit. For apart from me you can do nothing."

JOHN 15:1–5 NLT

UNDERSTAND:

- *What good fruit are you producing in your life right now?*

- *What ways can you improve on staying connected to Jesus, the Vine?*

APPLY:

Jesus described Himself as a vine and God the Father as the gardener. We are the branches. The fruit we grow on our branches are the good things we do for God that He has planned for us—the work He created us for, serving and giving to others, sharing God's love, and helping others to know Jesus as Savior. And we can't produce any good fruit unless we stay connected to Jesus, the vine. If you are feeling worn out and unproductive and like you're spinning your wheels at times, there might be an easy answer: you might need to check your connection to Jesus. Humbly ask the loving gardener to show you any problems and nourish you back to nearness with Jesus. God can make you thrive again with lots of good fruit growing on you!

PRAY:

Heavenly Father, please nourish me in my connection to Jesus, the vine. Help me to stay connected and grow the good fruit You want me to. Amen.

God Sees

READ PROVERBS 15

KEY VERSE:

The eyes of the Lord are in every place, watching the bad and the good.
PROVERBS 15:3 NLV

UNDERSTAND:

- *There is so much pithy, practical wisdom to apply in Proverbs. What verses in chapter 15 have great impact on you tonight?*

- *When you're tempted to give a harsh word but instead hold your tongue and give a soft answer, what happens? Do you practice this discipline regularly?*

APPLY:

No one has vision like God does. The Bible says He sees and knows absolutely everything in every place. "No one can hide from God. His eyes see everything we do. We must give an answer to God for what we have done," says Hebrews 4:13 (NLV). And Job 28:24 (NLV) says, "He looks to the ends of the earth, and sees everything under the heavens." For people making bad choices and living lives of careless sin, those verses might be scary. But for those who love and want to follow and obey God's Word, they are wonderful and encouraging. God wants us to obey His good ways because He loves us and wants what's best for us. Trust that He always sees you in every moment of your life, and let that give you peace and courage that He's able to strengthen and encourage you at any time and in any situation.

PRAY:

Heavenly Father, please remind me that You are always watching me in every place, in every moment, in every situation. Please let that truth encourage me and give me peace! Amen.

Choose What Is Better

READ LUKE 10

KEY VERSES:

As Jesus and his disciples were on their way, he came to a village where a woman named Martha opened her home to him. She had a sister called Mary, who sat at the Lord's feet listening to what he said.

LUKE 10:38–39 NIV

UNDERSTAND:

- *Do you relate more to Mary or Martha? How? Why?*

- *"It will not be taken away from her," says Jesus in verse 42. What does that remind you about the things of this temporary world versus spiritual, everlasting life?*

APPLY:

Martha was very good at hosting and knew all the details of planning and preparing for visitors. Since Jesus was such an extra-special guest, she wanted everything to be perfect for Him. But Martha grew very frustrated with her sister because when Jesus arrived, Mary didn't help her with the work of hosting. She simply sat at Jesus' feet to listen to everything He had to say. Both sisters loved Jesus and were showing it in their own ways. But Jesus lovingly told Martha that Mary had chosen what was best, to not fuss much over the details of hosting Him and to simply enjoy His company and listen to His teaching. We women all need that loving, gentle reminder from Jesus at times—to stop fretting and simply relax in the life-giving words and love of our Savior.

PRAY:

Loving Savior, I want to show my love to You in extra-special details, like Martha, but I want to always choose the best way by enjoying simply being with You and listening to You, like Mary. Please help me to balance this in my life. Amen.

Job's Prayers of Praise and Repentance

READ JOB 1–2

KEY VERSES:

He said, "Without clothing I was born from my mother, and without clothing I will return. The Lord gave and the Lord has taken away. Praise the name of the Lord." In all this Job did not sin or blame God.

JOB 1:21–22 NLV

UNDERSTAND:

- *What stood out as most familiar to you in the story of Job? What stood out as something you'd never heard of or thought much about?*

- *Are you holding on to any angry words or attitudes toward God of which you need to repent?*

APPLY:

Job's faith in God was tested in such an incredibly hard way. It's difficult to even imagine the pain and sorrow he endured. Yet after losing so much, Job "fell to the ground and worshiped" (Job 1:20 NLV). However, if you read the whole book of Job, you will find that Job was tested even more, but he did not continue to praise God through it all. In fact, he had quite angry words for a while. In the end, after God reminded Job of His greatness and goodness, Job cried out in repentance, "I hate the things that I have said. And I put dust and ashes on myself to show how sorry I am" (Job 42:2–6 NLV). Like Job, when we cry out to God with angry words, we should stop and realize God's power and love over all things in ways we cannot understand. And we must say we are sorry for our disrespect to God. After Job repented, God blessed him again even greater than before.

PRAY:

Heavenly Father, help me to have faith and strength like Job through grief, pain, and hardship. Help me also to learn from Job that if I speak in anger to You, I must apologize and continue to trust in You. Amen.

Who Can Compare?

READ ISAIAH 40:12–31

KEY VERSES:

"To whom will you compare me? Or who is my equal?" says the Holy One. Lift up your eyes and look to the heavens: Who created all these? He who brings out the starry host one by one and calls forth each of them by name. Because of his great power and mighty strength, not one of them is missing.

Isaiah 40:25–26 NIV

UNDERSTAND:

- *What is most overwhelming you right now?*

- *Have you felt God give you new strength when you needed it as you trusted in Him?*

- *What aspects of life and nature most remind you of how incomparably awesome our Creator God is?*

APPLY:

Life feels overwhelming sometimes, and when it does, let our amazing God overwhelm you even more. Isaiah 40 reminds you of His unmatched awesomeness. Who else is anything like Him and His greatness, majesty, and power? Absolutely no one! Our whole huge planet is like a tiny grain of sand in His hand. It's hard for our minds to fathom the incredible descriptions in this passage. And while some verses in Isaiah 40 could be interpreted that God is cold and uncaring toward all that He reigns over, the final lines of the chapter assure us that He is not. He is the almighty, unrivaled Lord of all, for sure, but He is also our compassionate and loving Savior for "He gives power to the weak and strength to the powerless. Even youths will become weak and tired, and young men will fall in exhaustion. But those who trust in the LORD will find new strength. They will soar high on wings like eagles. They will run and not grow weary. They will walk and not faint" (Isaiah 40:29–31 NLT).

PRAY:

Heavenly Father, please overwhelm me with Your magnificence, especially when I feel overwhelmed by life. I choose to focus on how You are sovereign over everything, and Your perfect plans will always prevail. Please give me new strength like You've promised, and remind me each day of how awesome You are. Thank You for being my great God and merciful Savior! Amen.

A Hungry Widow

READ 1 KINGS 17

KEY VERSE:

"As surely as the Lord your God lives," she replied, "I don't have any bread—only a handful of flour in a jar and a little olive oil in a jug. I am gathering a few sticks to take home and make a meal for myself and my son, that we may eat it—and die."

1 Kings 17:12 NIV

UNDERSTAND:

- *Have you ever chosen to provide for someone else with everything you have, trusting God alone to provide for you?*

- *In reading verses 17–18 and the widow's questions to Elijah, what do you think happened to her faith and attitude by that point? What did she soon experience and learn despite that?*

APPLY:

When the prophet Elijah found the widow just like God told him to, she told him she didn't have any bread—just a little bit of flour and oil. She was sure that she was about to make the very last tiny meal for her son and herself and that they would soon starve to death. Maybe you have experienced that kind of desperate resignation, either physically or spiritually. But God can make a way of provision and rescue, like He did through Elijah for the widow of Zarephath. She obeyed the instruction from God through His prophet and chose to trust that He would continue to provide for her and her son, even while she provided for Elijah first. Later, she was rewarded even greater when her son had died and Elijah brought him back to life through the power of God.

PRAY:

Heavenly Father, even when things seem utterly hopeless, remind me that You have the power to provide, restore, and heal in extraordinary ways. Fill me with peace because I trust and hope in You! Amen.

No Fakes

READ PSALMS 115–116

KEY VERSES:

Our God is in the heavens. He does whatever He wants to do. Their gods are silver and gold, the work of human hands. They have mouths but they cannot speak. They have eyes but they cannot see. They have ears but they cannot hear. They have noses but they cannot smell. They have hands but they cannot feel. They have feet but they cannot walk. They cannot make a sound come out of their mouths. Those who make them and trust them will be like them.

Psalm 115:3–8 NLV

UNDERSTAND:

- *What fake gods are most popular in today's culture?*

- *Are you ever tempted to worship a fake god? How do you fight that temptation?*

APPLY:

This scripture compares our one true God with the fake gods of the world that some people make for themselves. It describes how silly those fake gods are, with useless mouths, eyes, ears, noses, hands, and feet. But people often make fake gods because they don't really want to serve or worship anyone but themselves. So, they will end up as useless and meaningless as those fake gods. But to trust, worship, and obey our extraordinary God is to live the life you were created for, with love, hope, and peace forever.

PRAY:

Heavenly Father, I want to trust and worship You alone! Please help me keep far away from fake gods. Please help me to keep living for You and sharing You with others. Amen.

God Is Able

READ EXODUS 14

KEY VERSES:

Then Moses stretched out his hand over the sea, and all that night the Lord drove the sea back with a strong east wind and turned it into dry land. The waters were divided, and the Israelites went through the sea on dry ground, with a wall of water on their right and on their left.

Exodus 14:21–22 NIV

UNDERSTAND:

- *What stood out as most familiar to you in the story of the parting of the Red Sea? What stood out as something you'd never heard of or thought much about before?*

- *What feels like your Red Sea that you can't seem to get across tonight? How is God sustaining you as you pray for and wait on His rescue?*

APPLY:

Can you put yourself in this scene? Just imagine the next time you're at a lake or beach that all the waters suddenly move aside and make a pathway for you to walk through. Our minds can barely comprehend it. Yet our God is able to do the most incredible miracles. Maybe tonight you're feeling like you're stuck at the edge of a sea of stress, needing to get across but with no way to do so. Your situation might feel hopeless, but don't ever give up believing in God's power and ability to come to your rescue in any way He chooses. Verses 29–31 say, "But the Israelites went through the sea on dry ground, with a wall of water on their right and on their left. That day the LORD saved Israel from the hands of the Egyptians, and Israel saw the Egyptians lying dead on the shore. And when the Israelites saw the mighty hand of the LORD displayed against the Egyptians, the people feared the LORD and put their trust in him and in Moses his servant." Likewise, remember that through your stressful situation, God has plans to show His mighty hand and bring more people to faith in Him.

PRAY:

Heavenly Father, forgive me when I think all hope is lost. That is never true when I trust in You. I believe You are able to come to my rescue in any way You choose. According to Your will and for Your great glory, please help me and bring more people to faith in You in the midst of this stressful situation. Amen.

Watching Over You

READ PSALM 71

KEY VERSES:

For You are my hope, O Lord God. You are my trust since I was young. You have kept me safe from birth. It was You Who watched over me from the day I was born. My praise is always of You.

PSALM 71:5–6 NLV

UNDERSTAND:

- *What are your earliest memories of being aware God was watching out for you?*

- *What times in your life has God seemed closest to you? Why?*

- *What times in your life has God seemed far away? Why?*

APPLY:

You've had lots of people in your life who have taken care of you over the years—parents, grandparents, husband, siblings, aunts and uncles and other relatives, friends, teachers, coworkers, school staff, coaches, doctors, nurses, and on and on. As an adult, you take care of yourself more, of course, but you still need plenty of people in your life to call on for help with all kinds of things. Ultimately, though, God is the one who constantly watches over you. Praise and thank Him for His extraordinary care. It is God working through all of those who take care of you and help you when you need it. And He will for all of your life, like Psalm 23:6 (NLV) says: "For sure, You will give me goodness and loving-kindness all the days of my life. Then I will live with You in Your house forever."

PRAY:

Heavenly Father, thank You so much for watching over me and guiding me through many people in my life. I trust that You will always provide the right people in the right places at exactly the right times when I need them. Amen.

Unapproachable Light

READ EXODUS 33:7–23; 1 TIMOTHY 6:13–16

KEY VERSES:

He who is the blessed and only Sovereign, the King of kings and Lord of lords, who alone has immortality, who dwells in unapproachable light, whom no one has ever seen or can see. To him be honor and eternal dominion. Amen.

1 Timothy 6:15–16 ESV

UNDERSTAND:

- *How do these passages in Exodus 33 and 1 Timothy 6 relate to each other regarding the glory of God?*

- *What does Exodus 33:20–23 tell you about God's love and care of His people?*

APPLY:

No one yet has ever fully seen God because He is so awesome and incredible that we people are just not able. He "dwells in unapproachable light." It's like trying to look at the sun. We know the sun is there and we can see it and all the good it does, but it's just not possible for our human eyes to look at it directly—it's just too much! Our eyes were not made to look at something so bright and magnificent. But someday, at just the right time, we will get to see God fully, and we will realize how awesome and powerful He is and always has been over everything in all creation. Until then, we keep on loving, following, and serving Him with great hope for our perfect forever in heaven.

PRAY:

Heavenly Father, even now on earth while I cannot fully see You, I trust that You are working and You are guiding me. It's amazing to know that one day I will see You fully! I live with great hope for my perfect forever with You! Amen.

Above and Beyond

READ LUKE 5:1–11; JOHN 21:1–14

KEY VERSES:

When He had finished speaking, He said to Simon, "Push out into the deep water. Let down your nets for some fish." Simon said to Him, "Teacher, we have worked all night and we have caught nothing. But because You told me to, I will let the net down." When they had done this, they caught so many fish, their net started to break. They called to their friends working in the other boat to come and help them. They came and both boats were so full of fish they began to sink.

Luke 5:4–7 NLV

UNDERSTAND:

- *What does Peter's first reaction to the miracle in Luke 5:8 tell you about his character?*

....

....

....

....

- *In John 21:7, Peter jumped out of the boat and into the water as soon as he realized it was Jesus. Do you think you would have done the same? Why or why not?*

....

....

....

....

....

APPLY:

In Luke 5, at the very beginning of Jesus' earthly ministry, He helped the fishermen catch far more than they could have imagined. They had just spent the whole night fishing and had caught nothing, but Jesus only had to say the words and suddenly the fish were everywhere—enough to break their nets and sink their boat! And in John 21, we read how Jesus did a similar miracle, and this time it was part of how He was showing Himself alive again after His death and resurrection. Both times, the disciples must have been so amazed and overjoyed—and especially so after they had believed Jesus to be dead! Don't ever forget that God is able to provide so much more than you can possibly fathom—including eternal life! Keep trusting Him and asking Him for everything you need.

PRAY:

Loving Savior, You go above and beyond to show how You love to provide. Thank You for meeting my day-to-day needs with plenty of extra blessing, and thank You especially for giving eternal life! Amen.

Perfect Peace

READ ISAIAH 26:1–19

KEY VERSES:

You will keep in perfect peace all who trust in you, all whose thoughts are fixed on you! Trust in the Lord always, for the Lord God is the eternal Rock.

Isaiah 26:3–4 NLT

UNDERSTAND:

- *Think about a time when the path ahead of you seemed rocky and steep, but you made it through. How did God smooth it for you? Will you trust Him to do that again?*

- *Do you sincerely search for and seek God both morning and night? What does that look like in your life?*

APPLY:

Make this song of praise, written by the prophet Isaiah, your personal worship to God. Own what it says in your life. *You* are surrounded by the walls of God's salvation. *You* are kept in perfect peace when you trust in God and fix your thoughts on Him. He is *your* eternal Rock! Are you struggling with pride or dealing with someone in your life who is arrogant? Let God do the humbling that needs to happen. He smooths out the rocky and steep paths ahead of you as you trust in Him, obey His commands, and sincerely seek Him. You might be feeling so discouraged over the evil that others do as they pay no attention to God, but remember that it is His job to defend you and prevail over the wicked—*and He will*, in His timing. Praise God for anything good that you have accomplished in your life, because it is ultimately from Him. And never forget that as you deal with pain and hardship, you can hold fast to the truth that "those who die in the Lord will live; their bodies will rise again" (Isaiah 26:19 NLT).

PRAY:

Heavenly Father, please help me to keep my thoughts fixed on You, and keep me in Your perfect peace! Remind me of the powerful truth from Your Word that puts my attention on who You are, my eternal Rock, and all You are able to do. Amen.

Dearly Loved in Great Detail

READ MATTHEW 10

KEY VERSES:

"Are not two small birds sold for a very small piece of money? And yet not one of the birds falls to the earth without your Father knowing it. God knows how many hairs you have on your head. So do not be afraid. You are more important than many small birds."

MATTHEW 10:29–31 NLV

UNDERSTAND:

- *What does it mean to be as shrewd as snakes and innocent as doves in verse 16?*

- *What person in your life knows and loves you the very best? How does it make you feel to praise God for knowing and loving you even better?*

APPLY:

Jesus was sending out the twelve disciples and calming their fears. He urged them not to be afraid of anyone who could kill or destroy the body but not the soul. Find peace tonight in this passage, trusting that God is watching over both your body and soul so protectively. He will never let any lasting harm come to a soul saved forever by Him. Plus, He knows every single detail about you—far, far better than even your closest loved ones—right down to the number of hairs on your head. Your family and friends surely know and love you, but they can't possibly know and love you like your heavenly Father who created you. Praise Him tonight like this: "You made the parts inside me. You put me together inside my mother. I will give thanks to You, for the greatness of the way I was made brings fear. Your works are great and my soul knows it very well. . . . Your eyes saw me before I was put together. And all the days of my life were written in Your book before any of them came to be" (Psalm 139:13–16 NLV).

PRAY:

Heavenly Father, help me not to fear anyone or anything. I fear only You with deep respect and love. You know and love me far better than anyone else, and I trust that I am constantly in Your protective care. Amen.

Sadness Turned to Joy

READ PSALMS 30–31

KEY VERSES:

"Hear me, Lord, and have mercy on me. Help me, O Lord." You have turned my mourning into joyful dancing. You have taken away my clothes of mourning and clothed me with joy, that I might sing praises to you and not be silent. O Lord my God, I will give you thanks forever!

Psalm 30:10–12 NLT

UNDERSTAND:

- *Have you experienced God taking what once brought you great sadness and turning it into joy? What happened?*

- *Do you put your thoughts, emotions, and prayer requests into written words like the psalms? What value do you find in that?*

APPLY:

Only our amazing God can take the worst kind of sadness, anger, or pain in our lives and turn it into such joy we feel like dancing. He might do that for us here on earth in certain ways, or we might have to wait until heaven, but He promises that He will. With every hard thing you might go through, you can choose to either let those things turn you away and pull you apart from God or trust His promises and grow closer to Him. The first choice will only make things worse, but the second choice will have you dancing with joy one day!

PRAY:

Heavenly Father, rather than turn away from and rebel against You, please help me desire a closer relationship with You when I am sad, angry, and upset. I trust that You will turn it all into total joy someday. Amen.

Overpowering Hope

READ 1 THESSALONIANS 4:13–18; JOHN 11:1–44

KEY VERSES:

We want you to know for sure about those who have died. You have no reason to have sorrow as those who have no hope. We believe that Jesus died and then came to life again. Because we believe this, we know that God will bring to life again all those who belong to Jesus.

1 THESSALONIANS 4:13–14 NLV

UNDERSTAND:

- *Why did Jesus say He was glad He was not there when Lazarus died?*

- *What does it say about Jesus that He wept even though He knew He was about to raise Lazarus back to life?*

APPLY:

Are you grieving tonight? Maybe you have recently lost a family member or friend, and the pain and sadness feel nearly unbearable. But even while you cry and ache and miss them in this life, you can have hope that overpowers the grief. If your loved one trusted Jesus as Savior, they will be brought to new life again like Jesus. You will see your loved one again and spend eternity together in heaven. That is an incredible comfort—and it should motivate us to share the good news of Jesus. Just like God does, we should want all people to be saved from sin and have the incredible hope of the resurrection.

PRAY:

Heavenly Father, I'm grateful for the hope You give us that, because Jesus rose to life, so will all who trust in Him as Savior. Please comfort me in my grief tonight, and comfort all who are grieving. Help me to share with many others that the one true hope of salvation and resurrection is found in You alone. Amen.

God Stands with You

READ 2 TIMOTHY 4

KEY VERSES:

The first time I was brought before the judge, no one came with me. Everyone abandoned me. May it not be counted against them. But the Lord stood with me and gave me strength so that I might preach the Good News in its entirety for all the Gentiles to hear. And he rescued me from certain death. Yes, and the Lord will deliver me from every evil attack and will bring me safely into his heavenly Kingdom. All glory to God forever and ever! Amen.

2 Timothy 4:16–18 NLT

UNDERSTAND:

- *How do you keep a clear mind in every situation, like 2 Timothy 4:5 instructs?*

- *Have you experienced a time when you felt like all other people abandoned you and only God was with you to help?*

- *What was Paul's attitude toward everyone who abandoned him?*

APPLY:

When no one else was there to help, God Himself was with Paul, protecting him and giving him power. And Paul trusted that God would keep away every sinful plan that any evildoers might have against him. Paul also knew that God would someday bring him into heaven forever, so he had nothing to fear. Paul wrote all this in his letter to Timothy, but all of it is true for you to trust tonight too. God never leaves you even when you feel like everyone else has. He will provide what you need in whatever ways are necessary. He is always standing with you in every circumstance.

PRAY:

Heavenly Father, I trust that no matter what happens in my life, You are always standing with me. Ultimately, You will always keep me safe because someday You are going to bring me into perfect paradise in heaven with You! Amen.

The Mighty Voice of the Lord

READ PSALMS 27–29

KEY VERSES:

The voice of the Lord is over the waters; the God of glory thunders, the Lord thunders over the mighty waters. The voice of the Lord is powerful; the voice of the Lord is majestic.

Psalm 29:3–4 NIV

UNDERSTAND:

- *How do these three psalms speak into your life and give you peace?*

- *In what concerns are you needing to clearly hear God's voice? Are you doing well to give His voice the most attention?*

APPLY:

With so much social media and the entire internet carried around on our phones in our pockets and purses, we have constant, sometimes overwhelming, input into our lives from all kinds of sources, opinions, and persuasions. This can be a good thing when used wisely and a terrible thing without limits. It's easy to let far too many voices speak into our lives, especially when sometimes the loudest worldly ones are the worst kind of influence. It can be a struggle to let God's voice be the one we give the most attention to. So, we have to constantly go to His Word, putting it above all other influence. Psalm 29 describes the great power of God's voice, and we can focus on this psalm as we ask God to speak more boldly and loudly into our minds and hearts than any other voice. He is our loving, guiding shepherd. We should constantly strive to know and listen to His voice and follow Him alone (John 10:27).

PRAY:

Heavenly Father, please speak boldly and clearly to me. I want to hear Your voice above all others. Please help me to use wisdom and limits on how much I listen to other voices, and help me to give Yours top attention. Amen.

So Dearly Loved

READ ROMANS 8:18–39

KEY VERSES:

Nothing can ever separate us from God's love. Neither death nor life, neither angels nor demons, neither our fears for today nor our worries about tomorrow—not even the powers of hell can separate us from God's love. No power in the sky above or in the earth below—indeed, nothing in all creation will ever be able to separate us from the love of God that is revealed in Christ Jesus our Lord.

ROMANS 8:38–39 NLT

UNDERSTAND:

- *What is causing you to groan the most these days? How does this scripture passage encourage you even while you groan?*

- *Have you ever felt separated from God's love? What caused you to feel that way? Do you believe the promise in this scripture that it's impossible to be separated from God's love, no matter what hardship you're going through?*

APPLY:

Sometimes you might find yourself or a loved one in a situation so hard and so confusing you have no idea how to even begin to talk to God about it or ask for His help. In those times, you can be so grateful for the Holy Spirit and the promise in Romans 8:26 that He helps you in your weakness. He goes to God for you with "groanings that cannot be expressed in words." He pleads for you according to God's will. How amazing to know that you are so incredibly loved that the Holy Spirit is begging for what is best for you and that God is working everything together for good for those who love Him and are called according to His purpose. The final treasure of this passage is the powerful promise that assures you that absolutely *nothing* can separate you from God's love. Close out your day with total confidence of how adored you are by your heavenly Father. Even as you sleep, trust that you are being prayed for by the Spirit and you are constantly connected to God's love.

PRAY:

Heavenly Father, let me relax in Your amazing love for me tonight. Thank You that nothing can ever separate me from it. Help me to remember that even while the problems of this world seem overwhelming and agonizing, You are working out Your perfect plans in the midst of them. I am Your dearly loved child, and I trust You! Amen.

Because You Are with Me

READ PSALMS 23–25

KEY VERSES:

The Lord is my Shepherd. I will have everything I need. He lets me rest in fields of green grass. He leads me beside the quiet waters. He makes me strong again. He leads me in the way of living right with Himself which brings honor to His name. Yes, even if I walk through the valley of the shadow of death, I will not be afraid of anything, because You are with me.

Psalm 23:1–4 NLV

UNDERSTAND:

- *When have you felt you've truly been in the valley of the shadow of death? How did you feel God's presence with you there?*

- *Do you feel hated by anyone like David clearly did in Psalm 25:19? How does this passage help give you peace about that situation?*

APPLY:

One of the most familiar and popular passages of scripture is Psalm 23. Its comfort and peace abound as we picture God caring for us like a good shepherd lovingly cares for his sheep. God never leaves us as He guides, protects, and provides for us, until one day we are safely home with Him forever in heaven. Psalm 24 goes on to praise God for His greatness, glory, and holiness, acknowledging that everything in the world is His. And Psalm 25 pleads with God for direction, protection, and forgiveness of sin, trusting that He gives it and is full of goodness to those who love and obey Him. As you end each day, the praise and prayer in the psalms are beautiful ways to turn your heart and mind to God, letting Him give you the peace you need to rest well and prepare for a new day full of His plans, provision, and mercy.

PRAY:

Heavenly Father, You are my loving Shepherd, and I want to follow Your leading in all things. Please gently prod me back where I belong when I stray from Your good paths and plans for me. Forgive me for my sin, and help me to obey You. Amen.

Use Your Time Wisely

READ ECCLESIASTES 3; EPHESIANS 5:1–21

KEY VERSES:

Look carefully then how you walk, not as unwise but as wise, making the best use of the time, because the days are evil. Therefore do not be foolish, but understand what the will of the Lord is.

Ephesians 5:15–17 ESV

UNDERSTAND:

- *What things most tempt you from doing what you should be doing?*

- *How are you actively disciplining yourself in regard to those things, and what blessing and reward are you noticing as you do?*

APPLY:

It's far too easy to get distracted or be lazy about doing the good work God has for us to do. There are just so many opportunities and options in the world! Those things aren't necessarily all bad, but we need plenty of prayer and discipline to prevent them from getting in the way of what's most important in our lives. Most important should be what Jesus said the greatest command is: " 'You must love the Lord your God with all your heart and with all your soul and with all your mind.' This is the first and greatest of the Laws. The second is like it, 'You must love your neighbor as you love yourself.' All the Laws and the writings of the early preachers depend on these two most important Laws" (Matthew 22:37–40 NLV). And so, we continue to ask Him to show us how to live carefully and wisely, making the best use of the time to use our gifts to glorify Him in what He has planned for us.

PRAY:

Heavenly Father, please help me to keep Your great commandments first in my life—loving You completely and loving others as myself. Then help me to manage my time and days wisely to bring the most glory to You. This is a prayer I'll need to keep praying repeatedly. Thank You for hearing and helping me. Amen.

God Faithfully Forgives

READ 1 JOHN 1:1–2:14

KEY VERSES:

If we say that we have no sin, we lie to ourselves and the truth is not in us. If we tell Him our sins, He is faithful and we can depend on Him to forgive us of our sins. He will make our lives clean from all sin.

1 John 1:8–9 NLV

UNDERSTAND:

- *How does it feel to hold on to and try to hide sin rather than humbly admit it to God and ask forgiveness and help?*

- *What does it mean to walk in darkness rather than in light?*

APPLY:

It's not fun to humbly admit the sinful things we've done, but we need to tell them to God. To pretend like we don't sin sometimes is ridiculous, because God knows anyway. He sees and knows everything about us, even every single thought we have. So, we must take time to confess and ask forgiveness for our sins rather than hide them or act like they're no big deal. Psalm 103:11–12 (NLV) says, "His loving-kindness for those who fear Him is as great as the heavens are high above the earth. He has taken our sins from us as far as the east is from the west." That should fill us with such gratitude and peace. Our heavenly Father loves us so much and never wants to hold our sins against us.

PRAY:

Heavenly Father, I confess ____________ to you today, and I ask for Your forgiveness. Thank You for being such a forgiving and good God who gives me endless grace and love! Amen.

Spread the Good News

READ ROMANS 1

KEY VERSES:

I am not ashamed of the Good News. It is the power of God. It is the way He saves men from the punishment of their sins if they put their trust in Him. It is for the Jew first and for all other people also. The Good News tells us we are made right with God by faith in Him. Then, by faith we live that new life through Him. The Holy Writings say, "A man right with God lives by faith."

ROMANS 1:16–17 NLV

UNDERSTAND:

- *How have you shared the Good News lately?*

- *What sometimes hinders you from sharing the Good News?*

APPLY:

Did you do anything you feel silly or embarrassed about today? Some of us seem to beat ourselves up more than others over those types of things, even though we've all been there, done that. But as Christians, the one thing we should never feel embarrassed or ashamed of is sharing the gospel of Jesus. We should all want to be able to say, like Paul did in Romans 1, that we are not ashamed of the good news that Jesus came to earth to live a perfect life and teach us, then died on the cross to pay for our sins, and then rose to life again and offers us eternal life too. When we share this good news with others, we spread God's power to save people from their sins. That should never embarrass us but rather fill us with satisfaction and peace that we are participating in God's purposes and doing the very best work.

PRAY:

Heavenly Father, help me to never be ashamed to share the gospel of Jesus Christ. Thank You for wanting to save all people from their sins! Please empower me and give me great peace as I help to spread the good news. Amen.

Practical Peace

READ HEBREWS 13

KEY VERSES:

Now may the God of peace—who brought up from the dead our Lord Jesus, the great Shepherd of the sheep, and ratified an eternal covenant with his blood—may he equip you with all you need for doing his will. May he produce in you, through the power of Jesus Christ, every good thing that is pleasing to him. All glory to him forever and ever! Amen.

Hebrews 13:20–21 NLT

UNDERSTAND:

- *Ponder Hebrews 13:2. Have you experienced a time when you showed hospitality to a stranger whom you believed was truly an angel?*

- *In what ways can faith and following Jesus get overly complicated unnecessarily?*

APPLY:

We have ultimate peace with God because of the righteousness we gain when we accept the work of Jesus Christ on the cross to forgive our sins. And we can have plenty of practical, everyday peace in life if we focus on and apply the good instruction given in God's Word—like in the closing of the book of Hebrews. Keep loving each other and showing hospitality, kindness, and compassion to one another, including strangers. Empathize with those who are imprisoned and in pain. Honor and respect marriage with faithfulness and no sexual immorality. Be content with the simple blessings that provide for our needs; do not constantly strive to gain wealth and possessions. Do good works and share with the needy. Respect and follow the example of good faith leaders. Remember there is nothing mere people can do to us, because God never leaves us or lets us down. And breathe deeply with gratitude for the strength of God's grace and the fact that we don't need to get caught up in any new faith fads. We can trust that Jesus Christ is the same yesterday, today, and forever.

PRAY:

Heavenly Father, I am so grateful for Your grace and the practical wisdom and instruction to follow in Your Word. Please help me not to overcomplicate life and faith but simply keep loving and obeying You. Please equip me with all that I need to do Your will, and produce in me, through the power of Jesus, everything that is pleasing to You. Amen.

Godliness and Good Health

READ 1 SAMUEL 16:7; 1 CORINTHIANS 6:12–18; 1 CORINTHIANS 15:35–58; 1 TIMOTHY 4:6–10; 1 PETER 3:1–6

KEY VERSE:

Train yourself to be godly.

1 Timothy 4:7 NLT

UNDERSTAND:

- *How does the comparison of our earthly bodies to our heavenly bodies in 1 Corinthians 15 help you have wisdom about health and appearance goals for your earthly body?*

- *How do you apply the wisdom of 1 Peter 3:1–6 to the culture you live in today?*

APPLY:

Let God's Word give you peace tonight in a world that focuses far too much on body image. Social media posts, TV, and magazine covers try to make you feel like you are not healthy enough, physically fit enough, pretty enough, and so on. But your heavenly Father wants you to know that "physical training is of some value, but godliness has value for all things, holding promise for both the present life and the life to come" (1 Timothy 4:8 NIV). In other words, maintain the right perspective about keeping your body in good health and appearance. That has value, for sure, and we should want to eat healthy foods, exercise, and take good care of our temples of the Holy Spirit. But we can easily go overboard and let the focus be on pride in ourselves and our looks rather than on honoring God with the care of our bodies. Fix your thoughts and goals on godliness and good health in honor and worship of the one who knows and loves you most of all, from the inside out. Remember that your earthly body, no matter how great it does or does not look and feel right now, is just temporary; but your soul will go on forever in a new heavenly body. And never give control to any other input telling you what you have to look or feel like to fit into the world around you.

PRAY:

Heavenly Father, I want my goals to be about godliness and good health, not worldly appearance and fitness and fashion trends. Please help me to listen to Your voice on these matters more than any other input, and help me to honor You above all. Amen.

Extraordinary Grace

READ MATTHEW 27:32–44; MARK 15:21–31; LUKE 23:26–43

KEY VERSES:

He said to Jesus, "Lord, remember me when You come into Your holy nation." Jesus said to him, "For sure, I tell you, today you will be with Me in Paradise."

LUKE 23:42–43 NLV

UNDERSTAND:

- *Matthew and Mark mention the two criminals crucified next to Jesus, but only the Gospel of Luke gives the details of one's salvation. Why do you think that is?*

- *Do you know someone who believed in Jesus as Savior in their very last moments of life?*

APPLY:

Never forget as you are praying for loved ones who are nonbelievers that God gives every possible chance to come to salvation. When Jesus was dying on the cross, one of the criminals dying next to Him believed in Him and asked Jesus to remember him. And Jesus promised that the criminal would be in paradise that very day when he died. This account shows how full of grace our extraordinary Savior is. He gives grace until even the very last moments of life, wanting everyone to believe in Him and accept Him as Savior. So, keep on praying for those friends and loved ones who do not yet trust in Jesus. Keep sharing God's love with them, because He wants to give them every chance possible to spend forever in paradise.

PRAY:

Loving Savior, thank You for the example of the criminal beside You who believed at the last moment. That gives me so much hope for people I know who don't yet trust in You. I will keep on sharing Your truth and love with them. Please turn their hearts to You! Amen.

New Heaven and New Earth

READ REVELATION 21

KEY VERSES:

"Look, God's home is now among his people! He will live with them, and they will be his people. God himself will be with them. He will wipe every tear from their eyes, and there will be no more death or sorrow or crying or pain. All these things are gone forever." And the one sitting on the throne said, "Look, I am making everything new!"

REVELATION 21:3–5 NLT

UNDERSTAND:

- *Why do you think God didn't give us more detail about what life will be like in the new heaven and earth?*

- *Do you think the details we're given in Revelation are more literal or symbolic? Why?*

APPLY:

The Bible gives us some description and detail but doesn't tell us a whole lot about what forever life in the new heaven and earth will be like, probably because our minds couldn't fully understand how awesome it will be. First Corinthians 2:9 (NLT) says, "No eye has seen, no ear has heard, and no mind has imagined what God has prepared for those who love him." But God's Word does tell us everything will be new and spectacular in its architecture and beauty. Even better, there will be no more death or sorrow or crying or pain. Our dear heavenly Father will wipe every tear from our eyes Himself. We will have total peace and joy forever, with God making His home among us. Incredible! A lovely way to end your day is to praise and thank God for the perfect paradise He is creating for you and fall asleep dreaming of what it might be like.

PRAY:

Heavenly Father, I know the new heaven and earth will be incredible. It's beyond anything I can imagine, but it's still so fun to dream about. I thank You and praise You for the perfect forever You are preparing for all who love You and trust Jesus as Savior. Amen.

God Gathers the Waters of the Sea

READ PSALMS 32–33

KEY VERSES:

The heavens were made by the Word of the Lord. All the stars were made by the breath of His mouth. He gathers the waters of the sea together as in a bag. He places the waters in store-houses. Let all the earth fear the Lord. Let all the people of the world honor Him.

Psalm 33:6–8 NLV

UNDERSTAND:

- *How does the truth in Psalm 32:7 give you peace tonight?*

- *How does the singing and music such as that in Psalm 33:1–3 bring you peace?*

APPLY:

Have you ever sat on the beach, just staring and thinking how incredibly endless the ocean seems? Yet this psalm describes how God can gather the water of the sea together as simply as if putting it all in a bag, as the NLV puts it. The NIV says as if in jars. Our one true God is so huge and powerful, so far beyond what our minds can imagine. Let that truth encourage you every day, because the same huge and powerful God who gathers up the waters so easily is the same huge and powerful God who can give you extraordinary peace and power for whatever you are facing. Rest well in that truth tonight.

PRAY:

Heavenly Father, I am amazed by Your greatness and power! If You can gather up all the waters of the earth and control them, I trust that You can gather up all my worries and fears and take them away from me. I know You will encourage me and give me peace. Thank You! Amen.

Built on and Rooted in Jesus

READ MATTHEW 7:24–27; LUKE 6:47–49; JEREMIAH 17:7–8; COLOSSIANS 2:6–10

KEY VERSES:

Just as you accepted Christ Jesus as your Lord, you must continue to follow him. Let your roots grow down into him, and let your lives be built on him. Then your faith will grow strong in the truth you were taught, and you will overflow with thankfulness.

COLOSSIANS 2:6–7 NLT

UNDERSTAND:

- *How do these four different scripture passages relate?*

- *In what active ways do you continue to strengthen your foundation and grow your roots deeper into Christ?*

APPLY:

If we're in the middle of a storm but have a solid structure in which to take refuge, we still have a strong sense of peace. But if we're caught in a tent in the middle of an open field when tornadoes pop up or we're in a shack on the sandy beach of a raging sea, anxiety prevails. And we sure don't build a trustworthy treehouse in a tree without strong roots. So, if it seems anxiety is prevailing too much in our lives, maybe we need to reevaluate and reinspect our shelters and foundations. Have we built on something solid that will last or on things that are weak and temporary? Are there any damages or cracks? Are we continuing to check and repair and strengthen our foundations if needed? Are we nourishing and growing strong roots? Everything of this world is shaky and fleeting, and only what is built strong on and rooted deeply in Jesus Christ and the truth of His Word will endure.

PRAY:

Loving Savior, please help me to constantly keep fortifying my foundation on You and growing my roots deeper into You. Show me the cracks and weaknesses, and help me repair and strengthen them. Please keep my faith strong and unwavering, no matter the storms of life. Amen.

We Do Not Lose Heart

READ 2 CORINTHIANS 4

KEY VERSES:

Therefore we do not lose heart. Though outwardly we are wasting away, yet inwardly we are being renewed day by day. For our light and momentary troubles are achieving for us an eternal glory that far outweighs them all.

2 Corinthians 4:16–17 NIV

UNDERSTAND:

- *What are the hardships weighing on you tonight? What do you need to cry out to God about them?*

- *How are you seeking God's power to keep you from losing heart and being defeated by your suffering? How are you being renewed day by day?*

APPLY:

Some days we feel exactly like verses 8 and 9 of this passage describe—hard pressed on every side, perplexed, persecuted, and struck down. Anyone who says the Christian life should be all good all the time clearly does not read their Bible entirely and in context! We should not run from or deny the hurts and hardships we experience. Feeling all of the awful weight and pain of them and grieving them before God are what leads us to remember the powerful truth in that passage: Yes, we are hard pressed, *but we are not crushed*. Yes, we are perplexed, *but we are not in despair*. Yes, we are persecuted, *but we are not abandoned*. Yes, we are struck down, *but we are not destroyed*. How is that possible? Because God will never leave us or forsake us. He holds us up and strengthens us through the power of His Holy Spirit living in us. Jesus suffered and died for us, and we grow closer to Him as we share in suffering. At the same time, we show off His eternal-life-giving power to others when we suffer but are never defeated—until one day in heaven when we learn the purposes of our hardships and we see the amazing rewards they were gaining us!

PRAY:

Heavenly Father, please help me to see the value in these hardships I'm experiencing. They help me to know and to show off Your power and love as You strengthen and uphold me. I trust that they are achieving rewards for me so awesome that my mind cannot even imagine them. I am fully depending on You alone, Father, and I love You! Amen.

When Courage Melts Away

READ JOSHUA 7:1–15

KEY VERSES:

So approximately 3,000 warriors were sent, but they were soundly defeated. The men of Ai chased the Israelites from the town gate as far as the quarries, and they killed about thirty-six who were retreating down the slope. The Israelites were paralyzed with fear at this turn of events, and their courage melted away.

Joshua 7:4–5 NLT

UNDERSTAND:

- *In what ways has God called you to be a leader?*

- *What have been the worst unexpected turns of events in your life? What has God taught you through them?*

APPLY:

Like the Israelites in Joshua 7, we too have had turns of events in life that make us feel like our courage has melted completely away. As difficult as it is, in those times, we must look back and see if our sin contributed to the awful turn of events. Sometimes not at all, because it's just the hardship and trials of life or a situation God is using to teach us and refine our faith. But sometimes our sin has led to the rough circumstances in which we find ourselves, and we have to admit that. The hard but necessary truth is, if we disobey God, He's not going to fill us with His blessings and good courage. But there is merciful truth that because of the sacrifice of Jesus, "if we confess our sins, he is faithful and just to forgive us our sins and to cleanse us from all unrighteousness" (1 John 1:9 ESV).

PRAY:

Heavenly Father, please help me to keep obeying You and Your Word and quickly ask forgiveness and make things right when I sin. I want to keep Your courage solid in me. I don't want it to melt away! Amen.

So That Others Can Hear You

READ ACTS 16:16–40

KEY VERSES:

They were severely beaten, and then they were thrown into prison. The jailer was ordered to make sure they didn't escape. So the jailer put them into the inner dungeon and clamped their feet in the stocks. Around midnight Paul and Silas were praying and singing hymns to God, and the other prisoners were listening.

ACTS 16:23–25 NLT

UNDERSTAND:

- *Do you feel like you've ever been judged or even imprisoned unfairly?*

- *What have you experienced during times of choosing to praise God anyway in the middle of suffering?*

APPLY:

Few of us could honestly say we'd start singing worship songs soon after unjustly being beaten severely and thrown into a dungeon. Yet that's exactly what Paul and Silas did. Hopefully, we never find ourselves in jail, but we can still learn from their experience about how to respond to awful hardship. Choose to praise God anyway, and—this is the key—be sure to worship confidently so that others can hear you. Let the awesome results of Paul's and Silas's faithful display inspire you. They were soon miraculously freed from prison and led the jailer and his whole family to faith in Christ. And who knows how many fellow prisoners were listening to them and what additional impact their bold worship had? Only God knows for sure, and hopefully He'll tell us in heaven someday. Meanwhile, especially in the midst of suffering, keep praising and giving credit to God for all good things in ways that others can clearly observe in your life. As you enthusiastically share your faith, trust that God is using you in beautiful and miraculous ways you can't even imagine to draw more people close to Him.

PRAY:

Heavenly Father, I want to choose to praise You in every awful circumstance. No matter what is going on around me, You are still good. You are still loving and looking out for me. You will save and rescue at exactly the right time, according to Your will. I will tell others of Your love and power and saving grace forever and ever. Amen.

Small Part, Big Power

READ JAMES 3:1–12; PSALM 34:13; PROVERBS 18:21; 21:23

KEY VERSE:

We all stumble in many ways. Anyone who is never at fault in what they say is perfect, able to keep their whole body in check.

JAMES 3:2 NIV

UNDERSTAND:

- *What ways have you observed the tongue being a fire causing great damage?*

- *When are you most tempted to use your words sinfully? What practical ways can you work toward avoiding sin in this way?*

APPLY:

Did you say everything perfectly in all your conversations today? The odds are that you probably did not. This passage in James 3 is comforting as it reminds us that we're not alone in the struggle to control our words. None of us is perfect at this. It's far too easy to spout off without thinking when angry or hurt. Certain people and certain stressors can trigger us into speaking in ways we know are wrong. Sometimes we simply just get tired and careless. Sometimes we use the excuse that we "just need to vent." But since God's Word acknowledges how hard it is to control our tongues, should we just give up trying? Of course not. Our words matter—a lot. They have great control and power, like a bit in a horse's mouth or a rudder on a ship. And they have great potential for evil, unfortunately. We should take this passage as a warning to stay vigilant to keep our tongues in check. As Christians, we should not have both praise to God and curses coming out of our mouths. And when we mess up, which we will, we should correct our words and seek forgiveness quickly. Mostly, we should make Psalm 141:3 (ESV) our constant prayer: "Set a guard, O LORD, over my mouth; keep watch over the door of my lips!"

PRAY:

Heavenly Father, please set a guard over my mouth, and keep watch over the door of my lips. I need Your incredible power to help me control my tongue, because I will fail far too often on my own. Please forgive me when I sin with my words, and help me to make things right with others whom I've hurt. Thank You for Your grace that covers me! Amen.

Powerful Pep Talk

READ JOSHUA 1

KEY VERSES:

"Study this Book of Instruction continually. Meditate on it day and night so you will be sure to obey everything written in it. Only then will you prosper and succeed in all you do. This is my command—be strong and courageous! Do not be afraid or discouraged. For the LORD your God is with you wherever you go."

JOSHUA 1:8–9 NLT

UNDERSTAND:

- *How is God specifically calling you to be strong and courageous right now?*

- *Are you thriving at meditating on God's Word day and night, or do you need to improve on this?*

- *So far in your life, how has God given you success for your obedience to Him?*

APPLY:

God had called Joshua to be the one who would lead His people into the Promised Land after wandering in the desert for forty years under Moses' leadership. And in Joshua 1, you can read the powerful pep talk God gave to Joshua to help him be the brave new leader. It's not just for Joshua though. This scripture is a powerful pep talk from God to you as well, in whatever situation you find yourself. You have the whole Bible, the complete Word of God, including accounts of the life, teachings, death, and resurrection of Jesus Christ, plus the many books that came after the Gospels to study, memorize, and meditate on. And you have the gift of the Holy Spirit living in you to instruct and guide you as well. So, just as God did for Joshua, let God lead you in the wonderful purposes He has for your life as you follow His Word with strength and confident courage.

PRAY:

Heavenly Father, thank You for guiding me through Your Word. Please help me to focus on it day and night and live a life of obedience to it. I believe that only then will I truly prosper and succeed. Thank You for being with me wherever I go. Amen.

If You Lack Wisdom

READ JAMES 1

KEY VERSES:

If any of you lacks wisdom, you should ask God, who gives generously to all without finding fault, and it will be given to you. But when you ask, you must believe and not doubt, because the one who doubts is like a wave of the sea, blown and tossed by the wind. That person should not expect to receive anything from the Lord. Such a person is double-minded and unstable in all they do.

JAMES 1:5–8 NIV

UNDERSTAND:

- *Do you consider your troubles an opportunity for great joy? How do verses 3–4 and 12 help encourage you in doing so?*

- *Do you have any sin to confess and forgiveness to ask for in light of verses 19–21?*

APPLY:

When we're feeling too much instability and turmoil rather than peace in our lives, we might need to stop and ask ourselves, *Have I been asking for God's wisdom? Do I have faith in God alone and believe that He gives wisdom generously? Am I accepting and applying His wisdom in my life?* Our best source of God's wisdom is the Bible. And James 1 goes on to urge us to never just listen to the Word; we must listen and then *do* what it says. When we follow and obey God's Word and continue in it all our lives, then we will be blessed—and we will have the deep, lasting peace that depends on our never-changing eternal God and not on our constantly changing earthly circumstances.

PRAY:

Heavenly Father, I greatly need Your wisdom in all areas of my life. Thank You for Your Word to guide me in it. Tonight, I ask that You show me exactly the right wisdom I need in my current circumstances. As I read and listen to Your Word, I don't want to forget it. Please help me to sincerely obey and live it out. Amen.

Our Source of All Comfort

READ 2 CORINTHIANS 1

KEY VERSES:

All praise to God, the Father of our Lord Jesus Christ. God is our merciful Father and the source of all comfort. He comforts us in all our troubles so that we can comfort others. When they are troubled, we will be able to give them the same comfort God has given us.

2 Corinthians 1:3–4 NLT

UNDERSTAND:

- *Have you ever felt crushed and overwhelmed beyond your ability to endure (verse 8)? How did God rescue you and comfort you?*

- *Can you say with confidence and a clear conscience that you have lived with a God-given holiness and sincerity in all your dealings (verse 12)?*

APPLY:

When you're all tucked in for the night, thank God for that cozy feeling, because it's a gift from Him. Yes, it might also come from your favorite soft pajamas and your pillows positioned just right, but ultimately even those are from God. The apostle Paul calls God the source of all comfort. Every bit of goodness you receive that eases your distress or weariness in any way is given by God to encourage, strengthen, and refresh you. And it doesn't stop with you. God calls you to share that comfort with others—maybe even with gifts like pjs and pillows but most importantly with the encouragement and peace that God filled you with at just the right time. Maybe your comfort came through a scripture God brought to mind on a really bad day or a straight-to-your-heart sermon on the radio when you were stuck in traffic. Maybe it came through a worship song repeated throughout your week or a friend who brought you coffee and cried and prayed with you. God shares His comfort in a zillion ways, both big and small. As you receive it, praise Him with gratitude and then spread it around generously.

PRAY:

Heavenly Father, I think back on this day and see the many ways You provided comfort to me when I needed it. Help me to always be aware those are blessings from You and to be filled with gratitude for how You care for the details of my life. Thank You for providing the dear people and the precious gifts that encourage, refresh, and comfort me. Help me to generously pass them on. Amen.

Honor and Praise Forever and Ever

READ PSALMS 145–146

KEY VERSES:

I will honor You every day, and praise Your name forever and ever. The Lord is great and our praise to Him should be great. He is too great for anyone to understand. Families of this time will praise Your works to the families-to-come.

Psalm 145:2–4 NLV

UNDERSTAND:

- *Is verse 4 of this passage a goal in your family? Do you strive to praise God and His awesome works and inspire the next generation of your family to do the same?*

- *Do you think your praise to God is great? How could it be even greater?*

APPLY:

Tonight, let these psalms of praise be as soothing as a bedtime bubble bath. Focus your thoughts on your heavenly Father, and sing and pray the words of Psalms 145–146 to Him. Thank Him for all His mighty acts and kindnesses and for the ways He is slow to anger. Feel His closeness because He is "near to all who call on Him, to all who call on Him in truth." Trust that He takes care of you and will destroy the sinful. Do not put your ultimate trust in people who will fail you at times; rather, remember that God alone will never fail you, and your hope in Him is sure. He is your Creator, Provider, Healer, Protector, Deliverer, and your faithful and loving King! If you fill your mind with this kind of truth over and over, there is no room for worry or fear. Let your mind relax in the truth of God's Word and enjoy sweet rest.

PRAY:

Heavenly Father, You are so great that no one can fully understand it, but I want my praise to You to be great as well. I want my mind and my mouth to be full of constant praise to You and empty of worry and fear. Oh, how I love You, Lord! Amen.

It Is Your Father's Good Pleasure to Give You the Kingdom

— READ MALACHI 3:6–12; MATTHEW 6:19–24; 19:21–30; LUKE 12:32–34; 1 CORINTHIANS 9:6–15; 1 TIMOTHY 6:6–10, 17–19 —

KEY VERSES:

"Fear not, little flock, for it is your Father's good pleasure to give you the kingdom. Sell your possessions, and give to the needy. Provide yourselves with moneybags that do not grow old, with a treasure in the heavens that does not fail, where no thief approaches and no moth destroys. For where your treasure is, there will your heart be also."

LUKE 12:32–34 ESV

UNDERSTAND:

- *Based on these passages, what should our view about money and gaining wealth in this world be?*

- *What ways have you been storing up treasure in heaven? What ways could you store up even more?*

APPLY:

Finances can certainly cause a lot of anxiety. So, tonight's readings are just a handful of the many scriptures in the Bible regarding money, which when heeded can bring financial peace. God's Word is clear that gaining worldly wealth here on earth should not be our goal. In fact, "the love of money is the root of all kinds of evil" (1 Timothy 6:10 NLT). Our goal should be to store up treasure in heaven. How? By giving back to God through good works and with generosity to care for others in need. If financial worries are plaguing you tonight, keep searching and studying God's Word on this topic, and keep asking Him for His wisdom. Let Him reveal where you might need to make changes in your finances and trust *Him* more instead of your own desires and plans. Thank Him for the ways He has already blessed you. Seek out and listen to advice from others you know who are both generous and wise with money. Most of all, remember that everything you've been given is from God, and you are simply a steward of those gifts. Manage them well, and be generous for His glory, and you will be blessed beyond measure.

PRAY:

Heavenly Father, please reveal to me and correct me where I need to make changes in my finances. I want to honor You with all my gifts and blessings and generously care for others in Your Name. Amen.

No One Else Like Jesus

READ HEBREWS 7

KEY VERSES:

We need such a Religious Leader Who made the way for man to go to God. Jesus is holy and has no guilt. He has never sinned and is different from sinful men. He has the place of honor above the heavens. Christ is not like other religious leaders. They had to give gifts every day on the altar in worship for their own sins first and then for the sins of the people. Christ did not have to do that. He gave one gift on the altar and that gift was Himself. It was done once and it was for all time.

HEBREWS 7:26–27 NLV

UNDERSTAND:

- *Have you experienced opposition for your faith in Jesus? How does this passage help you handle opposition to your faith?*

- *How do verses 23–25 help give you great peace and gratitude?*

APPLY:

Throughout your life, people will challenge your faith in Jesus Christ and try to dissuade you, but belief in Jesus as God and the one and only Savior is the only religion that is right and true. We should share our faith peacefully and lovingly, never forcefully. Jesus alone was perfect and holy and without sin. He gave His own life once for all people of all time, and no other religion offers that kind of gift and love and miracle! To know Jesus as Savior is to simply believe in Him and accept the awesome gift He gave of grace and eternal life. He took our sins away when He died on the cross for them and then rose to life again. Hold fast to this awesome truth, and let God fill you with peace as you trust in Him.

PRAY:

Loving Savior, thank You for giving Your life to save everyone who believes in You! There is no one else like You! You are God and You are Savior, and I am so grateful for You! Amen.

Ready for Every Good Work

READ 2 TIMOTHY 2

KEY VERSES:

In a wealthy home some utensils are made of gold and silver, and some are made of wood and clay. The expensive utensils are used for special occasions, and the cheap ones are for everyday use. If you keep yourself pure, you will be a special utensil for honorable use. Your life will be clean, and you will be ready for the Master to use you for every good work.

2 TIMOTHY 2:20–21 NLT

UNDERSTAND:

- *How does verse 13 fill you with peace?*

- *Do you do a good job of obeying verse 16? How could you improve?*

APPLY:

Timothy tells us we should want to be a special utensil for God to use in the most honorable ways. But what does it mean to do as verses 19–21 describe? How do we keep ourselves pure and our lives clean? Verse 22 goes on to instruct us how when it says, "Run from anything that stimulates youthful lusts. Instead, pursue righteous living, faithfulness, love, and peace. Enjoy the companionship of those who call on the Lord with pure hearts." As the NIV puts it, we should "flee the evil desires of youth and pursue righteousness, faith, love and peace, along with those who call on the Lord out of a pure heart." Each of us must ask God how to best apply this in our own lives and circumstances and trust that He will show us where He wants to clean up our lives and correct us. The most rewarding and fulfilling way to live is to be ready for your Master to use you for every good work He has planned for you.

PRAY:

Heavenly Father, please constantly show me what areas of my life need cleaning up. Help me to run far away from temptation and evil. I want to be used in the beautiful ways You created me for. Amen.

Even Though the Ship Will Go Down

READ ACTS 27:18–28:2

KEY VERSES:

"But take courage! None of you will lose your lives, even though the ship will go down. For last night an angel of the God to whom I belong and whom I serve stood beside me, and he said, 'Don't be afraid, Paul. . . . God in his goodness has granted safety to everyone sailing with you.' "

ACTS 27:22–24 NLT

UNDERSTAND:

- *What stresses in life make you feel like your ship is going down? Have you experienced a total shipwreck? How did you see God rescue and provide?*

- *How has God brought you the most peace and encouragement to keep you moving forward after a big failure in life?*

APPLY:

Paul was a prisoner on a ship in a horrible storm, and his words to the crew and other passengers were somewhat comforting but very unsettling too. We might wonder, *Why didn't God just stop the storm? Why let them shipwreck at all?* But we must remember that God has never promised to always protect us from shipwrecks—literal or figurative. Yet even in the midst of them, He can save our earthly lives. And what He does promise is heavenly life forever when we trust in Jesus as our one and only Savior. Just as God promised, eventually Paul and everyone on board the ship were safe. And we see how God provided for their needs through the good people of the island they landed on. This account helps give us peace when we feel our own ships are going down. Even when they do, God will always provide the people and resources we need to survive and then lead us on a new course according to His will.

PRAY:

Heavenly Father, I don't always understand why we have to endure "shipwrecks" in our lives. But I know You rescue according to Your will and ultimately save and give forever life to everyone who believes in Your Son. Thank You for always providing for my needs and bringing me aid in every hard situation. Amen.

The Lord Reigns

READ PSALMS 97–99

KEY VERSES:

The L*ORD* *reigns, let the nations tremble; he sits enthroned between the cherubim, let the earth shake. Great is the* L*ORD* *in Zion; he is exalted over all the nations.*

PSALM 99:1–2 NIV

UNDERSTAND:

- *What ways have you experienced the truth of Psalm 97:11?*

- *As you engage in discussion of current events, do you help promote to others total trust and peace in God?*

APPLY:

It's hard to find the right balance of staying informed about current events without becoming overly anxious about them. The other extreme is to be totally apathetic about them, which is tempting with all the conflict and animosity among people with differing views. So, we need much prayer for God's wisdom and peace in the midst of them, and most of all we need to focus on God's sovereignty. Psalms 97–99 give us a healthy perspective. When we choose to praise God as King of all kings and sovereign Lord over all nations, we can be filled with unwavering peace regardless of any turmoil in the nations, leadership, and politics around us. We must trust that God is in control, and as 1 Timothy 2:1–4 (NLT) says, we also must "pray for all people. Ask God to help them; intercede on their behalf, and give thanks for them. Pray this way for kings and all who are in authority so that we can live peaceful and quiet lives marked by godliness and dignity. This is good and pleases God our Savior, who wants everyone to be saved and to understand the truth."

PRAY:

Heavenly Father, please give me wisdom and a healthy perspective as I try to stay informed about current events in the world around me. I praise You as King of kings and Lord of lords. You will judge all nations with justice and fairness. Please fill me with Your perfect peace as I trust in Your total sovereignty. Amen.

Peace in Our Troubles

READ ROMANS 5

KEY VERSES:

We are glad for our troubles also. We know that troubles help us learn not to give up. When we have learned not to give up, it shows we have stood the test. When we have stood the test, it gives us hope. Hope never makes us ashamed because the love of God has come into our hearts through the Holy Spirit Who was given to us.

Romans 5:3–5 NLV

UNDERSTAND:

- *What is a trouble you have gone through that you look back and are thankful for because of the way it strengthened you and your hope for the future?*

....

....

....

....

....

- *Who in your life needs to hear the message of salvation and hope in Romans 5? How can you share it with them?*

....

....

....

....

....

....

APPLY:

Nothing is stress-free in life. Even a perfectly planned, all-expenses-paid vacation in paradise will have moments of anxiety, at least here and there. We don't need to go asking for trouble, for sure, because it will gladly come our way uninvited. But rather than constantly trying to avoid and prevent it in our lives, we need to realistically expect it and proactively decide what to do with it. Romans 5 helps us think of trouble in a healthy, positive way. We can learn to be glad about it by remembering that it helps us learn not to give up and strengthens our hope that things will be better in the future. When our hope is in the right place—in God who has saved us through His Son, and has given us His Holy Spirit now and eternal, perfect life in heaven for the future—we will never be ashamed or defeated. Just as God sent His Son to save us at just the right time, He will always deliver us out of any trouble at just the right time.

PRAY:

Heavenly Father, help me not to run away from trouble but rather face it with the right perspective. You use stress and problems to help me learn to depend on You and to not give up. You have saved me through Your Son, and You are my ultimate hope and peace, dear Father. I trust You and praise You! Amen.

The Heroes Who Have Gone Before Us

READ HEBREWS 11

KEY VERSE:

They were longing for a better country—a heavenly one. Therefore God is not ashamed to be called their God, for he has prepared a city for them.

HEBREWS 11:16 NIV

UNDERSTAND:

- *Which of the faith heroes described in Hebrews 11 do you relate to the most?*

- *Do you feel like a foreigner and nomad here on earth? Why is that important?*

APPLY:

We have to admit, sometimes we do get weary of keeping the faith. We wonder why God isn't answering a specific prayer or creating the breakthrough we think we need or proving Himself exactly like we want Him to. We sometimes have doubt and need to be honest about it. In those times, Hebrews 11 is such a powerful chapter to read to revitalize you. It defines what our faith is—being sure of what we hope for and certain of what we do not see—and gives us an incredible overview of so many heroes who've gone before us holding to their faith. This reminds us and inspires us to keep on believing and being obedient to God, like they did, even when we can't see all of His plans or the final result. If you are ever tempted to give up the faith, open your Bible to Hebrews 11. Read and reenergize. Think of how you'd like your name to be remembered among your family and friends and generations as one who never gave up on God. Though we cannot see all that He is doing right now, we absolutely will one day soon.

PRAY:

Heavenly Father, please strengthen my faith in You as I remember the heroes of old who never gave up on You. Thank You for their examples in Your Word. Please remind me every day that I am looking to and living for a place far, far better than this world—the heavenly home where You make all things right and good. Amen.

Courage for Christ's Return

READ MATTHEW 24:30–51; 1 JOHN 2:15–29

KEY VERSES:

The Spirit teaches you everything you need to know, and what he teaches is true—it is not a lie. So just as he has taught you, remain in fellowship with Christ. And now, dear children, remain in fellowship with Christ so that when he returns, you will be full of courage and not shrink back from him in shame.

1 John 2:27–28 NLT

UNDERSTAND:

- *Do you feel any anxiety or peace thinking about Christ's return?*

- *How do you stay ready for Christ's return at any moment?*

APPLY:

As Christians, we are supposed to be ready for Jesus to return to earth at any time. Some people have great fear and anxiety for that event, but those of us who stay close to Jesus should be full of courage and excitement if we are strong in our relationship with Him. Waiting for His return should fill us with great joy and hope! Yes, there will be hardship in this life and in the end times as the Bible clearly describes, but our salvation and confidence in Christ are what give us deep and constant peace through it all. We must hold fast to that salvation and confidence in Christ and continue in persistent close relationship with our Savior. As we do, we'll be setting the example for others, and we'll help bring them to salvation and peace because of Jesus Christ too. There is nothing better than knowing the Way, the Truth, and the Life and leading others to Him as well!

PRAY:

Loving Savior, please keep me close to You. Help me to be disciplined in spending time with You and wanting more and more good fellowship with You! Keep me full of hope, courage, and excitement for Your victorious return; help me to inspire others to know and have perfect peace in You too! Amen.

About the Author

JoAnne Simmons is a writer and editor who's in awe of God's love and the ways He guides and provides. Her favorite things include coffee shops, libraries, the Bible, good grammar, being a wife and mom, dogs, music, Disney World, punctuation, church, the beach, and many dear family and friends—but not in that order. If her family weren't so loving and flexible, she'd be in big trouble; and if God's mercies weren't new every morning, she'd never get out of bed.